WALK IN LOVE

By

Mila Rayot

authorHOUSE™

1663 LIBERTY DRIVE, SUITE 200
BLOOMINGTON, INDIANA 47403
(800) 839-8640
WWW.AUTHORHOUSE.COM

First published by AuthorHouse 04/12/05

ISBN: 1-4208-3398-7 (e)
ISBN: 1-4184-8874-7 (sc)
ISBN: 1-4208-1052-9 (dj)

Library of Congress Control Number: 2004098769

Printed in the United States of America
Bloomington, Indiana

This book is printed on acid-free paper.

Cover illustrated by Mike Foley

Graphic design by Kathy Romano

Edited by Lalitha Iyer

CONTENTS

IF YOU FORGIVE THOSE WHO SIN AGAINST YOU, YOUR
HEAVENLY FATHER FORGIVE YOU. BUT IF YOU REFUSE TO
FORGIVE OTHERS, YOUR FATHER WILL NOT FORGIVE YOUR
SINS.

19

DO NOT LAY YOURSELVES TREASURES ON EARTH, BUT
LAY UP YOURSELF TREASURES IN HEAVEN.

23

WHOEVER WISHES TO BE MY FOLLOWER MUST DENY HIS
VERY SELF, TAKE UP HIS CROSS AND FOLLOW IN MY STEPS.

27

ALL SCRIPTURE IS INSPIRED BY GOD AND IS USEFUL FOR
TEACHING, FOR REPROOF, CORRECTION, AND TRAINING
IN HOLINESS SO THAT THE MAN OF GOD MAY BE FULLY
COMPETENT AND EQUIPPED FOR EVERY GOOD WORK.

31

YOUR LIGHT MUST SHINE BEFORE MEN SO THAT THEY MAY
SEE GOODNES IN YOUR ACTS AND GIVE PRAISE TO YOUR
HEAVENLY FATHER.

35

IF A PERSON IS WITHOUT FAULT IN SPEECH HE IS THE
MAN OF FULLEST SENSE, BECAUSE HE CAN CONTROL HIS
ENTIRE BODY.

39

I AM THE VINE, AND YOU ARE THE BRANCHES. HE WHO
LIVES IN ME AND I IN HIM, WILL PRODUCE ABUNDANTLY,
FOR APART FROM ME YOU CAN DO NOTHING.

43

STAY AWAKE! YOU DO NOT KNOW THE DAY YOUR LORD IS
COMING.

45

FAITH IN THE HEART LEADS TO JUSTIFICATION,
CONFESSION ON THE LIPS TO SALVATION.

47

YOU MUST BEFRIEND ONE ANOTHER, AS CHRIST
BEFRIENDED YOU.

51

I MYSELF AM THE LIVING BREAD COME DOWN FROM
HEAVEN. IF ANYONE EAT THIS BREAD HE SHALL LIVE
FOREVER, THE BREAD I WILL GIVE IS MY FLESH FOR THE
LIFE OF OF THE WORLD.

55

PRAY IN A SPIRIT OF THANKSGIVING

59

WHOEVER DIVORCES HIS WIFE AND MARRIES ANOTHER
COMMITS ADULTERY AGAINST HER, AND THE WOMAN
WHO DIVORCES HER HUSBAND AND MARRIES ANOTHER,
COMMITS ADULTERY.

61

GOLD AND SILVER ARE TESTED BY FIRE, AND A PERSON'S
HEART IS TESTED BY THE LORD.

67

ASK, AND IT SHALL BE GIVEN TO YOU, SEEK AND YOU
SHALL FIND, KNOCK AND IT SHALL BE OPENED TO YOU.
FOR EVERYONE WHO ASKS RECEIVES, AND HE WHO SEEKS,
FINDS, AND TO WHOM WHO KNOCKS IT SHALL BE OPENED.

71

SEEK TRUE PEACE, NOT UPON EARTH, BUT IN HEAVEN, NOT
IN MEN, NOR THINGS CREATED, BUT IN GOD ALONE.

75

WE STRUGGLE AND WORK HARD BECAUSE WE HAVE
PLACED OUR HOPE IN THE LIVING GOD, WHO IS THE SAVIOR
OF ALL AND ESPECIALLY OF THOSE WHO BELIEVE.

77

BLEST ARE YOU, WHOSE INIQUITIES ARE FORGIVEN AND
WHOSE SINS ARE COVERED OVER.

ACKNOWLEDGEMENTS

I wholeheartedly thank God for everything that He has done for me. Jesus Christ is my strength, my life, and my brilliant light. He is the source of wisdom and a fountain of grace. I see His greatness in every situation I encounter. I always remember the number of times I have been comforted through the difficult storms of life. Paths are not always straight or smooth. Roads are not always bright. Whether the pathways are wide or narrow, straight or crooked, as a Christian I try to arm myself with love. Love never fails. Love—creates, inspires, heals, and illuminates. I am thankful for the gift of life, and the gift of faith through which I am able to serve. With each act of faith, love, kindness, and compassion, introduce values that can change lives. Everything is more beautiful when it is share with love. I give thanks to God always, call in His name, and reach out to all nations what He has done.

INTRODUCTION

This book is dedicated to the young at heart who are seekers of true faith and love of Jesus Christ. There are warm words of encouragement, to learn by frequent reading of the Holy Scriptures and accompanied by prayers. So that God and man may talk together. For we speak to Him when we pray, we listen to Him when we read the divine sayings.

Jesus had given command in the text quoted to teach and to observe all that He had commanded. Now the gospel is not an ideology but aims at creating new life, the subject matter of teaching oral and written, contribute to the holiness of the people of God. Through the inspiration of the Holy Spirit the human words are at the same time, word of the Holy Spirit.

The word of God is the power of God, for the salvation of all who believe. To seek Christ in every event, see Christ in every man, whether neighbor or stranger. Imitating the humble Jesus, He does not desire honors but seeks to please God rather than man, ever ready to leave all things and to suffer persecution for justice's sake. Accept it in its fullness, and keep it in its purity with the most absolute fidelity.

When the spirit of truth comes, He will guide you into all truth... (John 16:12). In this way there is growth, which progresses to attain an ever deeper understanding of the spiritual things; constantly moving to the fullness of divine truth which is the word of God.

For God so loved the world, that He gave His only Son to show more clearly that His love is unconditional, by loving enemies by loving sinners. That is the theme of love. God's love in unconditional and He never stops loving anyone. When people sin even if they fall into hell, it's not because God stopped loving them but because they refused to be open and receptive to His love. God is love and he who abides in love abides in God and God in Him.

Love is the most precious gift that can be given to someone, a gift that cannot be bought. Love springs from a pure heart and good conscience. Love rejoices, not in unrighteousness but rejoices with the truth. Love patiently accepts all things.

We accomplish this not through our own power, but by offering ourselves to His infinite compassionate love. When we believe in the power love and our inmost unlimited capacities to give, life can take on a vast joyfulness. Love is the medicine for the sickness of mankind.

I began to trust love, to have faith in love, to develop a taste for it, and to look for it and find it in others, because it is based on understanding, which is the highest refinement of the virtue of charity. We must exercise toward ourselves—patience, kindness, gentleness, meekness, and warm understanding.

Moreover we see that Christ love is understanding, trusting, non-possessive, freedom-giving and redeeming love. But if so far as we are able to love without conditions, to that extent we share in God's unconditional love, we become more and more fully the beautiful diamonds, the beautiful person that God has made. In order to become a "diamond" we must continue to reach holiness. God's greater glory is the glorification of His compassionate love.

In Christ we see that His love is completely unconditional. Everything is seen as an expression of God's love, a color of God's love. To be lost is to live in an unregenerate condition, loveless and unloved, and to be save is to love, because God is love.

Love is a feeling which is lasting, kind, unfading to its hope and unselfish. Love never fails. Love is success, love is happiness, and love is life.

Love thinks no evil, imputes no motive, and sees the bright side in every action. What a delightful state of mind to live in!

Nothing in this world is perfect and unforeseen events are bound to happen in any situation. But love conquers all! We know from the scripture that God's love by its very nature, a redeeming, creating, compassionate giving love.

Love strengthens our steps in the right direction even through difficult paths. Without love life turns empty and bitter. There is no place of misunderstanding when goodness exists, because goodness is a wide open space for everyone to be.

If we want to enhance goodness in the world, we must strengthen the power of love—to give room to all that is good, beautiful and true. Each day offers us opportunities of sharing our love and concern. Every opportunity we miss will never come back!

LOVE DOES NO WRONG TO ANYONE, THEREFORE LOVE IS THE FULFILLMENT OF THE LAW.

Romans 13:10

Love is patient, love is kind. Love is not jealous, it is not snobbish. Love is never rude, it is not self seeking, it is not prone to anger, and neither does it brood over injuries. Love does not rejoice in iniquity but rejoices with the truth. It always protects, always trusts, always hopes and always perseveres. (1 Corinthians 13:4-7).

We are true Christians only through love. Love defines the word Christian. We must perfect ourselves in love. For true love cannot be a thing for the moment. It is eternal. God teaches us that. All true love is a reflection of Divine Life. True love for Jesus is never selfish. Love always shares. Love always finds a way to serve. For real love means action and service. We only really live when God lives in us, and there is no true love without the love of God as beginning, middle and end. This alone can withstand trials and temptations.

We do this in obedience to God's command, to please God and because God loves all men. Loving people who are good is not charity. The test of charity is in loving people who do not appeal to us. It is easy to serve agreeable characters. It is charity to serve disagreeable characters.

In addition, our love to others ought to be universal, not excluding anyone—loving all, the good and wicked, those who love us as well those who hate us, strangers as well as friends. We must also give Him our whole heart without any reservations whatsoever, for He is ineffable goodness and source of all good. To do the will of God is therefore a concrete expression of our love for Him. Each day must find us with greater devotedness to our fellowmen in all our acts. Each day must see us grow in prayer, in lowliness of heart, in love with others. If we truly adore God, we must submit ourselves entirely to His rule. We are ready to do His will in all things, just as our Master did. Loving God in Himself and loving our neighbor that is the goal in life. By subjecting our intellect to God and believing what He has revealed.

In a word it is our obligation to live for Him, not for ourselves, to offer ourselves entirely to Him and to His divine service. To search in all things His greater glory, in short, we must love Him and serve Him without any restriction and limitation. When we concentrate ourselves both soul and body to His service for life, we are not performing some extra-ordinary work, we simply fulfill our duty of most strict justice.

Let us acquire good manners, and be polite and courteous to all. We should avoid uncharitable words and thoughts, and a spirit of faultfinding. We should be unselfish, and have regard for the right of others. Let us take every opportunity of doing a good turn to our neighbors.

If we make an effort to see God in everyone we shall find out that people are interesting, friendly, and lovable. We must bear and wear a sincere love by forgiving others whatever grievances we have against one another, forgive as the Lord has forgiven us.

Let us ask the Lord to pour His love in our hearts, to be patient to others and have a steady heart to conquer evil by doing good, because only when we love with God's love shall we love sincerely, unselfishly, warmly and perseveringly our neighbor. Christ said: If you love me keep my commandments (John 14:15). Well, let us do the best we can. Let us often say, "You, O Lord, have done so much for me, I will do this at least for love of You.

Dear Jesus thanks for Your love. You redeemed me by Your precious Blood. You have been good enough to let me know, how much You value my soul, and that I mean a lot to You. Let me always remember Your love, and let that memory hold my heart from every least sin, and keep my soul in every way and forever Yours. Amen.

YOU SHALL LOVE THE LORD YOUR GOD WITH YOUR WHOLE HEART, WITH YOUR WHOLE SOUL, WITH YOUR WHOLE MIND, AND WITH YOUR WHOLE STRENGTH, AND YOU SHALL LOVE YOUR NEIGHBOR AS YOURSELF.

Matthew 22:37-39

There are Ten Commandments. The message is love of God and love of fellowmen. God is calling us to fall in love with Him with our whole heart, mind and strength. We must seek God first. He is first in our thoughts, first in our hearts, and first in our lives for Him, and love Him best of all and better than anything in the world.

By loving God we mean acting out our lives in doing His will, loving Him before everything else, for His own sake. We shall love Him with a burning love, and we shall be undaunted with unspeakable happiness. Loving God in this way on earth is a foretaste of future glory in heaven.

As we remember the word of scriptures: It is not those who call me Lord, will enter into the kingdom of heaven, but the person who does the will of my Father.

It was clear then that loving God was not only a matter of feeling but of will. It means not saying things, but doing things, small and great to make Him happy, to give Him pleasure. Perfect obedience on the other hand, requires us to obey everything. It means God in everything and everything for God.

We are called to live in God's love, to experience gratitude to God and rejoice in Him and all of His gifts. Knowing ourselves and seeing our sinfulness in the light of God's love. It involves a healthy attitude toward self, a good self-image. At the heart of our life with God is turning to Him, being radically open to Him, falling in love with Him. God is calling us to know and experience Him in a more profound way, to be faithful to Him in daily prayer. We can give our hearts to seeking God and praising Him, and receive the new word the Lord has for us this very day. We can allow Him to enlarge our hearts. We need to decide to live totally for God before prayer makes sense.

To seek the kingdom of God is to seek the glory of God and our salvation. This is what we seek above all else. Jesus is the straightest way, the sovereign truth, the true life, the blessed life, and everlasting life.

It is a great thing to be obedient, for it is better if the will of God be so, that we suffer for doing good than for doing evil. For this is the will of God that we keep His commandments. As we live for Christ, our love grows more complete, so we will not be ashamed and embarrassed at the Day of Judgment but we can face Him with confidence and joy, because He loves us and we love Him too.

Be on guard against every form of immorality and keep a close watch on ourselves in everything we do, and discipline ourselves in all our conduct. Keep in mind the commandments of God and never let them be erased from our heart. We have to walk all our life on the path of righteousness. Loving the name of the Lord and becoming His servants. True happiness is found in God alone. God has this promise.

Dear Jesus, how tenderly You love me! For I know that in Your divine wisdom and love, You will arrange everything for the best. Grant me the gift of Your divine love, that I may ever love You with my whole heart, mind, and soul. Help me to serve You without condition and never cease in my praise. Amen.

LOVE YOUR ENEMIES, PRAY FOR YOUR PERSECUTORS.

Matthew 5:44

Jesus teaches us to lead in love. Jesus proves His love for us. Love your neighbor as yourself. Do this and you shall live (Luke 10:25-27). Love your neighbor as you love me. As often as you did it to the least of my brothers, you did it to me. Love one another as I have loved you. There is no greater love than this to lay down one's life for ones friends (John 15:12-13).

Perfect love union with God that they may be one as we are one, I living in them, you living in me. (John 17:20-23). As the father loves me I love you... live on in my love (John 15:9). Because of His great love for us He brought us to life with Christ when we were dead in sin (Ephesians 1:7). Jesus says; you are precious in my eyes and I love you. (Isaiah 43:4).

Jesus came into the world to teach us in reality that God is a personal God who loves. Jesus reaches out in love to everyone, to those who accepted His love, and to those who rejected the love He offered. He taught us that the most important commandment was to love. This love is based on the truth that abides in us and will be with us forever (2 John 1:6).

To love God is to know Him and to share His life. We must be willing for the love of God to suffer all things... "Love surrender's all." The most important thing is to love in whatever event and circumstances in our past, present, and future. Do not then surrender your confidence, it will have great reward (Hebrews 10:35).

In doing our service to the Lord, let us remember His word saying: My son, when you come to serve the Lord, prepare yourselves for trials, and in (2 Timothy 3: 12) He says: Anyone who wants to live a godly life in Christ Jesus, can expect to be persecuted. His message reminds us in (1 Peter 4:12). Do not be surprised beloved, that a trial by fire occurring in your midst it is a test for you, but it should not catch you off guard In (Hebrews 10:33). At times you were exposed to insult... you may suffer in distress of many trials, because men will be lovers of self and money, abusive, disobedient, hating good and lovers of pleasure etc. (2Timothy 3:4) rather than God.

Sometimes we are accused, we are judged, we are condemned, we are put to humiliation, we are victims of hate, gossip, insult, we are criticized and we are cursed, etc. It will cause us, to suffer much. What we are going to do is let us be patient with them, because our Lord's Patience directed toward salvation. God will not forget our work and the love we have shown Him by our service, past and present to His holy people (Hebrews 6:10). Rejoice instead in measure that we share Christ suffering.

Every action and understanding, every life that is good and truly Christian, bears the double sign of love and sacrifice. Our love must be strong and sincere enough, to think that suffering is normal and even desirable. There at the cross and only there, to love means to suffer. When suffering is an act of love, one can never take offense or be overwhelmed by it.

Trials always dismay us. We get over one trial, but the next one finds us again shocked and dismayed. For there is always another, "yes," God is so great. His name is Jesus Christ, and we believe it. We are not to love trials, but to love to follow Christ even if it means suffering.

Humility is based on faith, wishing to receive everything from God, light as well as strength—a humility which calls us to follow Jesus, walking in His steps, doing what He does. God is not honored by mere lip service. He said to Jews once: This people honors Me with their lip but their hearts is far from Me. (Matthew 15:8). To obey is to love—it is the loftiest, most adoring—perfect act of love.

Faith is the foundation and root of the whole spiritual life. To live by faith is to consent to live by God's promises. What it means, to accept everything. Furthermore,the more faithful we grow, the more God's grace tries our faith to perfect it. We often take more severe test and we are tempted to complain. But if we are truly living by faith, God calls us to be more and more complete. The faith that demands so much strength, which we must work hard to develop, is the gift of God.

The grace of perseverance is the grace of all graces, for which must incessantly appeal to God. Only love can overcome our faint heartedness, and learn to imitate the unconquerable steadfastness of Jesus. Recall the word of Jesus in the garden of olives, and see that He was reluctant to drain to the dregs the chalice of bitterness.

However, Jesus remained there in His agonizing prayer, struggling against the inclination of His Human nature, which offered stubborn resistance, doing such violence of His human feelings to bring about the bloody sweat. Reflect on that scene. We must draw courage from this example of the perseverance of Jesus, so as not to give up at the sight of difficulties, but go on till we have attained the object of our struggle. The grace of perseverance is a particular gift of God which enables us to continue in the state of grace until death comes.

Even when Jesus was dying on the cross, His enemies invited Him to give up His perseverance, and come down. They even tempted Him with the bait of His promised "conversion." Let Christ the king of Israel, come down from the cross, which they may see and believe. (Mark 15:32). In spite of this, He did not give up His purpose, but remained nailed to the cross till His death to accomplish our redemption. Difficult though it may seem perseverance—is also the most important of virtues. What is the value of even a long life of fervor and sanctity, if it is finally ruined by failing to persevere to the end? A Christian must not pay so much attention to his beginning, but coming to a successful end, for the reward is reserved only for the one who fights resolutely till the end. Whoever perseveres into the end will be saved. (Matthew 10:22). Only the one who reaches the goal. Now our prize in heaven the crown of life that the eternal Father is preparing as a reward for our fidelity, but without perseverance we cannot gain this crown.

Fellow Christians, let us make the cross the anchor of our lives. In the cross is salvation! In the cross is life. Therefore, though we suffer, we must easily forgive, willingly yield to others and be humble. We know that in following our Divine Savior and denying ourselves, we will receive a hundredfold reward and eternal life.

We plead not merely to be enabled to fulfill God's will, but to love His commands. Let us remain faithful until death that we may be given the crown of life. Let us place this precious gift in the service of Christ.

Dear Jesus, in all the ups and down of this world, I need You. I know You will deliver me from evil and help to bear my crosses. Help me to make You the glory of my life inside my soul, and in my dealing with others. So give me the grace to appreciate You as I should and by making You my "glory." Allow me to carry the light of Your revelation to each and everyone I meet. I want to give it all to You for Your honor and glory. Take it and keep it please forever. Amen.

I AM THE WAY, THE TRUTH, AND THE LIFE, NO ONE COMES TO THE FATHER EXCEPT THROUGH ME.

John 14:6

The grace of God our savior has appeared to all men, instructing us, in order that rejecting ungodliness and worldly lusts, we may live temperately and justly and piously in this world, looking for the blessed hope and glorious coming of our great Savior Jesus Christ.

In His act of creation, God gave each one of us a mind and a free will. These are the endowments of our immortal soul. We possess these gifts, not of our physical appearance but because of the spirit which is in us. We are the only creatures on this earth who can think and judge and freely choose. Great talents but equally great responsibility! How are we using our talent? Our mind must seek the object for which it was created, and the proper object of our mind is the truth. We must strive at all times and at all cost to seek the truth. We should know that the purpose of our mind is to seek Jesus, because He is truth itself.

Christ assures us to hear His words, to seek the truth, to listen, to put into work, in order to achieve holiness that God requires. As Christian we follow Christ. Jesus said: "Come and follow me." To follow Christ means to follow the way of thinking of Christ, the value which gives meaning to the life of Christ and what Christ stands for. When we begin to pay attention to ourselves we are in danger. We stand to become sad. We tend to bend on our own efficiency.

Let us try to approach, as much as we can the mind and heart of Jesus Christ as it is found in the gospel. We have the opportunity to get closer to Jesus, not in a hollow sentimental way or emotional way, but closer to Him in spirit. That is His way of thinking and looking at things.

The renewal should have been a renewal of spirit, a renewal in truth, a renewal over the patterns of Christian living, which is Jesus Himself the word of God. God has given us the power of expressing our thoughts in words and thus passing them on to other people. If our words and actions correspond with our inward thoughts, then, we are truthful and trustworthy.

Truthfulness is something very valuable. God Himself is infinite truth. Truthfulness makes us noble and worthy of respect, it is a solid foundation for trust and certainty among men. That is why God requires us that we must be truthful.

A truthful person is one whose outward speech and action correspond with His inward thoughts. We must be truthful because God is truthful, because truthfulness makes us noble, because truthfulness leads others to trust us.

Untruthfulness is a very great evil. The liar is imitating the devil whom our Lord called "the father of lies" (John

8:44). He greatly displeased God. Lying corrupts character, ruins trust, and causes much evil in the world.

It is true that human nature is prone to evil and that at time we are influenced by passion. But now coldly and analytically, we should settle the matter and admit that if there is one serious occasion of sin that we will not relinquish, we are not truly and truthfully following Jesus.

Keep close to Jesus in our ways. But now we are matured physically and mentally. We stand today in the eyes of God as grown men, adult women. And can we say that the grain of faith received in our soul so early in life, has reached the stability and the maturity of a strong tree. When it grows up it... becomes tree, so that the birds of the air come and dwell in the branches. We have a further duty than just of ourselves. It is true that our primary purpose in life is to save our own soul, and that strong tree of faith and good works can accomplish that. But we have the obligation towards others, that of charity and good example. These are the birds of the "air" who wants to dwell in the branches.

The followers of Christ—the Christian belong to the kingdom of truth. God is truth. And the virtue of truthfulness is the image of Divine Truth. God defines truth through Jesus and the Bible. For the word of God is living and powerful. It changes people's lives, thoughts, directions and behaviors. Truth is freedom. Truth is power. Truth is eternal. The God of truth is the God of life.

Our highest desire is for a full knowledge of truth and enjoyment of goodness. But God is the highest goodness, and therefore we should find our happiness in knowing and loving God as much as we can.

Let us at once detach ourselves entirely from all the things of this world, and thus secure a powerful help to perseverance.

Dear Jesus, how glad I am that I know You, and all Your goodness and all Your love for me. That is the greatest gift of all the gifts You have given me. Please give me strength to follow You without condition and limitation. Keep me as Yours, everyday of my life, until I become Your keepsake in heaven forever. Amen.

IF YOU FORGIVE THOSE WHO SIN AGAINST YOU, YOUR HEAVENLY FATHER FORGIVE YOU. BUT IF YOU REFUSE TO FORGIVE OTHERS, YOUR FATHER WILL NOT FORGIVE YOUR SINS.

Matthew 6:14-15

Does God forgive sin? Come now, let us set things right says the Lord; though your sins be like scarlet they may become white as snow, though they be crimson red, they become white as wool. If you will obey me, you will eat good crops from my land. But if you refuse to obey and if you turn against me, you will be destroyed by your enemies' swords. The Lord Himself said these things.

Let us read the gospel on the parable of the Prodigal Son; (Luke 15:11-32), the incident on the story of Mary Magdalene; (Luke 7:36-50). In relating the story the prodigal son and the adulteress Mary Magdalene, Jesus shows us how God forgives. As soon as a person realizes his sins and turn to God, God opens His arm and receives that person in His love.

God is loving, compassionate and forgiving. Can we who are constant recipients of His mercy be harder and more proud? We must remember that God does not forgive us because we deserve forgiveness, but because He is good and He loves us.

Mila Rayot

God showed the beautiful example of forgiving us which lead us to forgive others. Forgiving the sins of our neighbor is an act of humility. Let the love of God to men be the basis of our love for our fellowmen. God would forgive us only in the measure that we forgive others from our hearts.

We must be ready to forgive with all sincerity and honesty, because God loves us first. If on earth we don't forgive our neighbors, then our Father in heaven won't forgive us when we are face to face with Him at the last judgment.

God's forgiveness to us is conditional—on the condition that we forgive others! Jesus asks us to forgive and He also assures us, "my burden is light." Forgiving frees us. Forgiveness makes life easier, not harder. Not forgiving restricts our sense of humor and our ability to enjoy life. And it weakens our love even toward those people we don't need to forgive.

God forgives completely and the matter is never brought to mind. God's Forgiveness is instant and infinite. However, we rarely forgive others. We should be more forgiving to our brothers and sisters, because we belong to the community of God the Father, Son, and the Holy Spirit. Being Christian we are ready to "forgive and forget." We should always open our hearts and be Christ to those who offended us.

Although, man has continually sinned from the start, Jesus is always there to forgive and forget, if we confess our sins to Him. When temptation comes around us, let us always remember Jesus, our point of reference, our model.

20

Forgiveness has to do with God's compassion, the pity which He has for man's weakness and misery. By the act of forgiving we can build the community of love; also by forgiving sinners you have given them a chance to lead a happy, peaceful life. An unforgiving spirit saps our creative energy, our capacity of fresh thinking. If we are involved in any manner of vengeance, whether by action or by attitude, we must stop now. This also means we apologize for what we have done. If we cannot forgive, we cannot love.

Everyday we are faced with opportunities to forgive others, and regardless of how often we are hurt or unjustly treated our Lord calls upon us for our unlimited forgiveness. We should be ready to shun off pride and forgive if others offers their apologies. In return we should ask forgiveness if we commit mistake.

It is difficult sometimes to forgive because we are just human, but if we pray to God through the help of the Holy Spirit we can do it. God's forgiveness comes from His loving mercy. In the same token our forgiveness should spring from our love for Him and love for His people.

The ability to forgive comes from proper relationship with God, which begins when we confess and repent of the time we hurt others—our own sins. We can forgive only one way: By letting go of our pride that stands in the way of forgiving.

In order to arrive at the truth, we must have a sincere desire to know the truth, and willingness of heart to obey Christ. Knowing Jesus personally, making Him our best friend.

So the important thing is to know Jesus personally as a friend. God the creator of love and forgiveness, we can change our attitude. Willingness makes all the difference. And if we are willing, God has a wonderful plan to make His law even more beneficial to us.

Dear Jesus, there is much in my life that has offended You. I am sorry for it all. Some of it was willful, some come from weakness. But I am sorry now, and I humbly ask Your pardon, and I know You will forgive and forget my sins, because of Your tender mercies. So, please help me the right thing to do. Amen.

DO NOT LAY YOURSELVES TREASURES ON EARTH, BUT LAY UP YOURSELF TREASURES IN HEAVEN.

Matthew 6:19-20

Christ said: What profit would a man if he gained the whole world and destroyed himself in the process? The Lord exhorts us to seek eternal treasures rather than temporal fortunes. While there is nothing wrong in acquiring wealth provided, it is in accordance to God's word, temporary possessions won't do us any good in heaven. On the other hand, it is good things that we do on earth that will earn us treasures in heaven. Even insignificant gestures like a kind word, a friendly smile, a helpful hand, always given with love and sincerity has great value in the eyes of the Lord. As our daily bread puts it, we are not made rich by what is in our pockets but by what's in our hearts. Then Jesus said: Keep from wanting all kinds of things you should not have. A man's life is not made up of things, even if he has many riches (Luke 12: 15).

In order to reach eternal life, we must live as children of God. We must do our outmost to avoid sin, and by means of good work earn merit in heaven. The Son of God became man and died on the cross, so that all mankind might be saved.

Therefore, we must earnestly desire the salvation of others beside ourselves.

We must take care of our eternal salvation, because our eternal salvation is the most important than anything else in the whole world. Seek ye first the kingdom of God and His justice (Matthew 6:33). Therefore everything that we do on earth ought to help in some way toward saving soul.

We should never put our eternal salvation in danger. Hence, we must never be concerned about our earthly happiness, as to damage our chances of eternal happiness. We have got to fight against our inclination to evil and overcome ourselves. We have to be ready to lose our fortune, our reputation, our freedom, even our life, rather than to risk our eternal salvation.

The joy for us to experience now is limited. People occasionally get sidetracked in their search for total happiness. So while there are ways to attain a degree of it in this life, it won't be total joy. Real joy is found in God alone. God has this promise.

Let us every morning present ourselves to God as little children, protesting that we live ourselves entirely in His disposal and accept freely whatever He may arrange for the day, submit in all things to His ever adorable will. Renew our offering with our dear Lord, saying: "thy blessed will be done" especially when we are overtaken by any calamity, trouble, or misfortune.

Let us convince ourselves on this great truth that as self will is the source of all evil, so in the accomplishments of God's will—is our true happiness and satisfaction.

Dear Jesus, my soul must be very valuable if You purchased it as such a high price. So, let me always and everywhere realize the value of my soul, and that it belongs to You. Help me to see and to do what is right—always and everywhere, that one day I may rise glorious with You. Amen.

WHOEVER WISHES TO BE MY FOLLOWER MUST DENY HIS VERY SELF, TAKE UP HIS CROSS AND FOLLOW IN MY STEPS.

Luke 9:23

There are times when God Himself not only permits the temptations of the enemy, but even tries us Himself by tribulations, pains, sickness, crosses and trials.

Suffering is an opportunity to become spiritually beautiful. Human life is a thorny bush climbing up the tree of the cross, embracing all the sorrows and duties and burdens of life. But God promises: Whoever loses his life on earth, will find true divine life. We know that sufferings in this world are not to be worthy compared to the joys of heaven.

Take up therefore our cross and follow Jesus, and we shall go into everlasting life. Our Lord Jesus Christ is not one hour of His life without suffering. The whole life of Christ was a cross and martyrdom, and the more the flesh is brought down by afflictions, the more the spirit is strengthened by inward grace.

For they who now willingly hear and follow the word of the cross, shall not then be afraid of eternal condemnation. This sign of the cross will be in heaven that's when the Lord shall come to judge. The cross is salvation, in the cross is life. In the cross is infusion of heavenly sweetness. In the cross is joy of spirit, in the cross is height of virtue, in cross is perfection of sanctity. There is no health of soul nor hope or eternal life but in the cross.

We must not therefore despair when we are tempted, but pray to God with so much fervor that He may vouchsafe to help us in all tribulations, who no doubt according to the saying of the Apostle Paul, will make such issue with the temptation that we may be able to bear it (1 Corinthians 10:13).

Temptation is not a sign of wickedness—it is actually a sign that you are right with God. In fact, the good often have greater temptations than others. Our Lord Jesus Christ permitted Himself to be tempted by the devil—to gluttony, to avarice, and to pride (Matthew 4:3). Briefly, the life of Christ was a life of sacrifice.

God permits us to be tempted, to try us and to give us a chance to merit heaven. God never tempts us, but when we resist temptation He rewards us. Temptation when resisted with constancy also purifies us, makes us humble and wins us new graces.

A thousand difficulties do not make one doubt, just as a thousand temptations do not make one sin. First rule in every temptation is pray. It is consoling to remember that the greatest servants of God have suffered temptation. They conquered them by prayer. God gives everyone the grace to do the same.

We are sure to find the cross of suffering, when and where we least expect it. Grief, pain, sorrow, humiliation, setback, and the like, are constantly entering into our life. We need not make difficult studies to learn how to derive profit from our sorrows. Jesus Christ our Lord was outstanding in this, and He has left us remarkable examples to imitate.

It is sufficient simply to consider the way in which the blessed Lord endured the rigors of poverty, pain and torture of soul and body. Nevertheless, see how patiently He suffered all these appalling tribulations.

Let us therefore humble our souls, under the hands of God in all temptations and tribulations, for the humble in spirit we will be saved and exalt. In sorrow and temptation, we should encourage ourselves to a virtuous life by the thought of our own resurrection.

As the risen Christ kept His wounds in His glorified body as a mark of what He had suffered, so the toil of pain we endure in the service of God will be an increase of glory for us in the next life. The more we suffer with patience, the greater will be our reward.

Let us prefer to lose all, even the most precious things in life rather than to give up our faith. Let us never be ashamed of the cross, remembering that all Christians are bidden to take up their cross and follow Jesus.

Let it be the final conclusion, that "through many tribulations we must enter the kingdom of God." And yet we know from our Lord's teaching that love for one another is as necessary as taking up our cross and following Him.

Dear Jesus, You suffered much during all Your life for me, and You died in terrible torments. You came down from heaven, lived a hard life on earth, and died a harder death on the cross. Thank you for the priceless gift of the forgiveness of my sins. So please help me to devout myself to You. I want to serve You without condition and limitation. Please help me to bear my crosses well, so that when You come to judgment I may stand on the right—among the saved. Amen.

ALL SCRIPTURE IS INSPIRED BY GOD AND IS USEFUL FOR TEACHING, FOR REPROOF, CORRECTION, AND TRAINING IN HOLINESS SO THAT THE MAN OF GOD MAY BE FULLY COMPETENT AND EQUIPPED FOR EVERY GOOD WORK.

2 Timothy 3:16

Christ assures us to hear His words, to seek the truth, to listen, to put into work in order to achieve holiness that God requires. Jesus said: "It is written: Man does not live by bread alone. Man is to live by every word that God speaks." (Matthew 4:4).

A quiet time of listening and studying the word of God is essential to our spiritual growth. The power of God's word can affect within us a complete transformation. As we feed at the table of His word, we will discover a change coming over us. Our relationship to others will gradually change. We may not ever perceive the transformation taking place within us, but His word is powerful and effective.

As we strive to draw near to God, we get a better insight into the tragedy of sin. Sin is the refusal to respond to God's love for us. As we listen prayerfully to His word, we become more and more experientially aware of His loving abiding presence within us. Our personal relationship with God develops, and we gradually acquire a fresh spiritual way of thinking. We develop a new mentality as our mind becomes conformed to the mind of Christ.

As we listen, God reveals more and more about Himself. He is a God who loves us with a creative, providential, forgiving, healing, and redeeming love. God's word is creative, powerful, encouraging, instructive, cleansing, and comforting. The closer we come to God, the more radically will our value system change; this relationship with God is fundamental to a life of prayer. Jesus invites us to follow Him, walk with Him. He makes us co-responsible with Him. Enjoy victory with Him. Celebrate with Him.

As we expose our thinking to His word, a real cleansing process takes place within us. We see how much of our thinking might be rationalizing. As we become transformed by His word, our self-centeredness begins to fade and our vision takes on the cosmic vision of Christ.

The word of God is to be our study. Christ is the truth. His word is truth. All the sayings of Christ have a value beyond His unpretending appearance. The Bible is God's great lesson book, His great educator. The foundation of science is contained in the Bible. Every branch of knowledge may be found by searching the word of God. And above all, it contains the sciences, the science of salvation. The true higher education is gained by studying and obeying the word of God.

—❤—

Dear Jesus, I want You to take possession of my heart. Whatever of self is there and whatever of human love, I want You to change it and make it Yours. So let me learn to love You each day more and more, in thought, word and deed. Give me grace to do this, please, because I want You to acknowledge me as Yours forever in Heaven. Amen.

YOUR LIGHT MUST SHINE BEFORE MEN SO THAT THEY MAY SEE GOODNES IN YOUR ACTS AND GIVE PRAISE TO YOUR HEAVENLY FATHER.

Matthew 5:16

Light produces every kind of goodness, justice, and truth. Light is the symbol of goodness and happiness. Hence, through our goodness we enjoy true happiness.

The way of wisdom leads directly to the light that grows brighter. Perfect wisdom is the fulfillment of the law. All wisdom comes from the Lord and in Him it remains forever. The first point of wisdom is to know what is true; the second to discern what is false.

The eyes are the body's lamp. If your eyes are good, your body will be filled with light. If your eyes are bad, your body will be in darkness. And if your light is darkness, how deep will the darkness be (Matthew 6:22-23).

Take care then that your light is not in darkness. The man who walks in the dark does not know where he is going (John 12:35). While you have light, believe in the light, so that you walk as children of light. But those who do what is right come to the light, so everyone can see that they are doing what God wants (John 3:21).

Jesus spoke to them once again: I am the light of the world...no follower of mine ever walks in darkness. He shall possess the light of life. If a man is walking by day he does not stumble because he sees the world bathed in light. But if he goes walking at night he will stumble since there is no light in him (John 11:9-10).

While we have the opportunity, let us do well to all men, and be continuing examples of love, faith, piety, integrity, steadfastness, gentle spirit, etc. Do not neglect good deeds and generosity, because the true servant of the Lord must not be quarrelsome but must be kindly towards all.

Therefore, devote our hearts and souls to seeking the Lord. We serve Him with perfect hearts and willing souls, and worship Him faithfully with our whole heart. Keep in mind the great thing He has done among us. Defer to one another out of reverence for Christ. We shall act faithfully and wholeheartedly in the fear of the Lord. Observe carefully all the commandments of the Lord, His ordinances and statutes.

All of us who are spiritually mature must have this attitude, and progress in the faith that we may be rich in the harvest of justice, until the coming of Christ. Our love may more and more abound both in understanding and wealth in experience, that we may attain full knowledge of His will through wisdom and spiritual insight. For it is our special privilege to take part—not only to believe in Him but also to suffer for Him.

For it is not those who hear the law who are just in the sight of God, it is those who "keep" the law who will be declared just. It shows that the demand of the law is written in our hearts. We must remember that we cannot hide from Him.

Yet the law is holy and the commandment is holy and just and good. Let the law be observed...so have courage and take action! Keep careful watch over our conduct. Do not continue in ignorance, but we try to discern the will of the Lord, and be filled with the spirit. We speak in Christ's name, pure in motivation; follow the way of love, even as Christ loved us. Be imitators of God and His dear children.

So, while we wait for the salvation that comes from Him, let us call upon Him to help us, and He will hear our cry if it is His good pleasure. Besides all this, we should be grateful to our God, for putting us to the test. God remembers His people and renders justice to His inheritance. God is gracious, compassionate, and forgiving, slow to anger and rich in mercy. His love is great!

Indeed, sorrow for God's sake produces repentance without regrets, leading to salvation—to bring it to successful completion, just as we are rich in good work, and total love to others.

Dear Jesus, I love You. You know it and I know it. But without Your sustaining omnipotence, I would drop back into nothingness. Give me such grace not to keep that light hidden, but rather to let it shine before all men, that they may come to know and love You better. And becoming an apostle of Your truth and love, by words, yes, but much more and always, and everywhere, by my life itself. Amen.

IF A PERSON IS WITHOUT FAULT IN SPEECH HE IS THE MAN OF FULLEST SENSE, BECAUSE HE CAN CONTROL HIS ENTIRE BODY.

James 3:2

God has given us our tongue to speak useful and kind words. If we use our tongue to lie or to abuse our neighbor we defile it. The Apostle James says: "If anyone is never at fault in what he says, he is a perfect man, able to keep his whole body in check. So let us keep a careful guard over our tongue, remembering that we shall have to give a strict account of every idle word. If we examine our conduct and inclinations, we shall discover it. Then let us labor and conquer it. In the morning we must resolve to avoid it during the day. In the evening before retiring, we should examine whether we have fallen into it, and if we have we should repent and renew our resolution. This practice continues day after day applied to all fault one by one, would soon root them and make us perfect.

If we wish to attain perfection, we must cultivate a habit of prayer; we must sanctify our daily actions, by offering them each morning to God. In this way all our actions, and even our recreation and sleep become a prayer provided of course, we live in a state of grace. The Apostle Paul says: Whether you eat or drink or whatever else you do, do all for the glory of God (1 Corinthians 10:31).

Each day we come in contact with many people—family, friends, teachers, employers and others. What we say, and how we say it, not only affects them but also affects us, either positively or negatively. But words once spoken cannot be taken back! Therefore, comfort and build up one another as you are doing (1 Thessalonians 5:11). Never let evil pass your lips, say only good things men need to hear, things that will really help them (Ephesians 4:29).

We should treat people the way we would like to be treated. This also has a benefit for us, because people tend to treat us the same way we treat them. Our manner of speech will often determine this: Being friendly, honest, and sincerely striving to encourage others, will tend to motivate them to do the same for us. Show concern for others, help and encourage them to do their best excel in all areas of life. By looking for good character traits in other people, we won't be quick to find and to point their faults and shortcomings. "Treat others the way you would have them treat you (Matthew 7:12).

Ask God daily for the wisdom to say the right thing at the right time. He will give us this kind of wisdom, if we sincerely desire it and trying to do those things that please Him (1John 3:22).

A person who is careful in what he says, will enjoy peace of mind and be blest in other ways, knowing that he has not offended others by careless or unkind remarks. So guard your mouth, try always to say the right thing at the right time. Be sure to think before you speak. "Faultless conversation calls for a great spirit of sacrifice and self-renunciation, together with an extra-ordinary self-control." So let God do it, trusting the Holy Spirit to work in your life.

Dear Jesus, You know that I really love You above all things. Look at my heart of love and my desire to serve. Lord, I praise You and I thank You for the gift of life, the gift of faith, the gift of joy, the gift of love, and the gift of peace that comes from You, the Divine Giver of all gifts. Teach me to pray, to love, to care, and to adore You forever and ever. Amen.

I AM THE VINE, AND YOU ARE THE BRANCHES. HE WHO LIVES IN ME AND I IN HIM, WILL PRODUCE ABUNDANTLY, FOR APART FROM ME YOU CAN DO NOTHING.

John 15:5

We can bring forth good fruit. The good fruit which Christ wants us to bring forth—and which He does everything in His power to promote—is holiness, which at final harvest will mean for us life- everlasting. This holiness is the rich colorful goodness of purity of life, courage, cheerful trust in God, patience, kind-heartedness toward our neighbor. We can only bear good fruit of holiness by doing the will of God.

We must first of all want to do God's will, and that we know is not always an easy one. It is the old story that we have so often heard. For the tree to bear good fruit, it has to expose itself to the sun, the rain, the wind, and to the pruning and cutting of the gardener. So, we must lay down ourselves often for God to work in us—the Sun of His love and its demands (especially when it requires love of neighbor). The wind of His will bends us almost to breaking; the pain of pruning, sickness, suffering of all kinds, separation from loved ones may seem well nigh unbearable. But these things are necessary for us. There is no good fruit without them.

Then, we must desire and resolve to do everything in our power to develop the divine life. Life we have received, to become more like unto Christ our Brother, the only begotten Son of God. We have to speak to Him, trust in Him, and walk with Him. We can maintain this contact by prayer: A prayerful state of mind will keep us in the right path of righteousness. This was Christ's way of keeping in touch with His Father all His Life. We should try to make it our way, too.

God is all perfect, all just, and all loving. He gives us our life. We return to Him not part of it, but all of it. Not some years, but all years, not some days but all days, not some moments, but all moments. Not some task, but all tasks, the greatest and the smallest. To go beyond keeping His commandments and take up His precious cross in self- dedication to all His interest, to think of nothing but His kingdom.

Dear Jesus, I want to come to You as You invite me and learn from You all I can, for You know everything and know it perfectly. Teach me above all, to love as a child loves its father with fear that is filled with love, and I shall be happy in serving You. Amen.

STAY AWAKE! YOU DO NOT KNOW THE DAY YOUR LORD IS COMING.

Matthew 24:42

Our Lord warns us to be watchful, placing before us our uncertainty as to when we shall die. He says to us: "The day is not certain. Be watchful!." Watch out for attacks from the Devil, your great enemy." He prowls around like a roaring lion, looking for some victim to devour (1 Peter 5:8). Therefore, we should be watchful with much carefulness! Wherefore, says the Lord, you also must be ready all the time, for the Son of Man is coming at an unexpected hour (Matthew 24:44).

Watch and pray that you may not enter into temptation (Mark 14:38). By that sentence Christ meant: Don't trust yourself, trust in God. We ought then to do good not for an hour merely, but always and continually. God requires us to obey His will always, for the reward for which we are looking is everlasting and unfailing. "If a man will set no limit to his labor, God will set no limit to the reward" (Galatians 6:9).

Moreover we should obey God as He deserves—promptly, energetically, and accurately. He requires us to obey Him with great firmness of will, so as to be able to overcome all difficulties that might arise. Look then at our model, Jesus, from whom we will learn this much needed courage and determination.

We should guard our eyes, ears, tongue, and hands carefully, because sin enters the soul by the five senses. We must always remember that our body is the temple of the Holy Spirit. Our consecration to the service of our King must be total and complete, comprehending all our faculties of body, of soul, of our whole life. All things belong to God. We must serve Him both by external and internal acts. We must be God-centered.

Then we will have true community life, with charity binding us together. We will serve Him with gladness and come before His presence with exceeding great joy, knowing that the Lord is God and we are His people and sheep of His pasture. Once again our Lord calls upon His followers not only to watch but to pray.

Dear Jesus, death is nearer and nearer each single moment. I need Your grace and peace every day of my life, and every moment of every day. There is so much turmoil and trouble in the world, and so many temptations and disturbances in my life that I find it hard not to get upset. I accept it from Your hands. May its end find me nearer and dearer to You, and so I beg You to keep me always far from sin by making me grow daily in Your love. Amen.

FAITH IN THE HEART LEADS TO JUSTIFICATION, CONFESSION ON THE LIPS TO SALVATION.

Romans: 10:10

Faith comes through hearing, and what is heard is the word of Christ. Faith is a precious gift and we thank God for it everyday of our lives. It can become weak. It can go stale. It can be lost. If we think of it as a bright flame, we know that it is for us to keep it bright and glowing. We do this by prayer and studying the word of God. Neglect of prayer means dimming that sacred flame. But the more we know about God, the more we love Him. Our life's ambition must be to imitate and resemble in some way the Lord Jesus Christ and to imitate and follow Him, seeing that He is the way that leads men to life.

By reading the gospel with loving attention, happy to take to heart all that Jesus says: The just shall live by His faith by seeing all things from the point of view of faith. Faith unites us to God and makes us share His thought and His life. Faith widens our knowledge of God and all the things of God. Faith is a source of comfort, not only in struggles for perfections, but also in all suffering, and sorrow. Faith is necessary to our salvation, and worthy of God's blessing and a source of merit.

Faith is not absent from truth, it is action—sacrifice. Love is not a passing physical thrill; it involves self-sacrifice in the word of Christ. The Apostle Paul writes: Not that we are sufficient of ourselves to think anything as of ourselves, but our sufficiency is from God (2 Corinthians 3:5). Faith is the greatest wealth on earth. Faith is the source of salvation. Faith is the foundation and root of justification. Just as a root, not only to sustain a tree, but also to provide nourishment to produce leaves, flowers, and fruits. So, faith not only to maintains spiritual life, but nourishes it by inspiring us to make acts of hope and charity.

Therefore, we continue to be confident. We know that while we dwell in the body we are away from the Lord. We walk by faith not by sight. We do not lose heart because our inner being is renewed each day, even though our body is being destroyed at the same time. The present burden of our trials is light, compared to the eternal life of glory that is beyond comparison. We do not fix our gaze on what we seen, but on what is unseen. What we see is transitory, what is unseen will last forever (2 Corinthians 4:18). Rather, let us profess the truth in love and grow to the maturity of Christ the head. Through Him the whole body grows and with the proper functioning of the members joined firmly by each supporting ligament, builds up in love.

Continue therefore, to live in Christ Jesus the Lord in the spirit which we received Him. Be rooted in Him and build in Him, growing stronger in faith, as we were sought, and overflowing with gratitude. Be on our guard, stand firm in faith. Do everything with love.

Dear Jesus, thank You for the great gift of faith. I promise to rely on Your grace to do what is necessary for my salvation. Please strengthen my faith, hope and love. So that I can serve You with my whole heart everyday of my life. Amen.

YOU MUST BEFRIEND ONE ANOTHER, AS CHRIST BEFRIENDED YOU.

Romans 15:7

Friendship is universal, as in Christ. Friendship within a community, even to outsiders is always the most striking and appealing fulfillment of our Lord's words. "By this everyone will know that you are my disciples if you have love for one another" (John 13:35).

Friendship is having... someone to talk with, someone to walk with, someone to share with, and someone to care with. A friend inspires, encourages, and gives heart to grow, helps to think more kindly, and to live more graciously.

The good kind of friend encourages, and supports your efforts with praise for every step along the way, and makes you believe you can grow. A friend is one who's there in good and bad times.

Good friends are a gift from God. True friends value each other highly and remain faithful both in joy and in sorrow; they pray for each other and help each other. Christ became our brother and our changeless friend, and loves us so much that He went to His death for us. Thus He shows us how much we should love our brothers, sisters, relation, and friends.

How can others help us? What can others help us to be or to become? Why others are able to help us? We can help others to become themselves for "no man is an island, no man stands alone." The Christian achieves psychological maturity, and spiritual perfection, and become the effective builder of a better world—like Christ; He is fully concerned, and responsive to the needs of others. What we are is God's gift to us. What we become is our gift to God.

We need people to help us, through word, deed and example. Grow and develop as persons, use our talent become creative and productive; become ourselves, because people want to share, because they care, because they love. So we must be concerned for their salvation. We should walk hand in hand with our brethren.

Yet, the greatest commandment is: Love your neighbor as yourself. This commandment is not fulfilled simply by giving physical, material help to our neighbor. As our own deepest need is spiritual, we love our neighbor truly when we seek to give them not only comfort for their body, but light and strength to their soul.

A busy life prohibits us from giving much time or thought to our fellowmen. Yet, all of them are in need, and our love should reach out to them. In Christ we are all one, and for that reason one with one another.

We can do more than just that: Love God with total love, and love our neighbor as ourselves. Then we will know what life and happiness and peace really are: We are to love God because He first loved us, and because He has saved us, and has kept us saved.

We must labor in planting and watering, but we must never forget that it is God who gives the increase. We must love others, because they are the objects of the intense love of God the Father, and because they are consecrated temples of the Holy Spirit.

In the new law our Lord has insisted on our loving not only friends, but our enemies, and both by word and example. We must beware of betraying any sign or trace of dislike, of impatience, weariness or anger—rather; we should strive to anticipate them with kindness.

Let us henceforth be truly earnest in our love of our enemies, doing well to those who hate us, and praying for those who persecute and calumniate us. For our Lord declares that it shall be rewarded by an infinite treasure in heaven, and possession of an eternal kingdom.

Let us therefore study to preserve and promote union and charity in ourselves and in others, to be patient and kind, such as bears all things, and endures all things.

Let us remember that we are not laboring for time, but for eternity. Not for man, but for God, for our neighbor's salvation. Not for an earthly, but heavenly reward, for God's greater glory, through love for Jesus Christ and in a spirit of loyalty to Him. Again, we should perform our duties in a spirit of diligence and humility.

—❤—

Dear Jesus, I often tell You to do what You want for my life. No matter what happens to me, no matter what goes wrong, I should be very happy because You have done marvelous things for me. Teach me to walk with faith, not by sight. Help me to pray fervently, and believe that nothing is impossible with You. Amen.

I MYSELF AM THE LIVING BREAD COME DOWN FROM HEAVEN. IF ANYONE EAT THIS BREAD HE SHALL LIVE FOREVER, THE BREAD I WILL GIVE IS MY FLESH FOR THE LIFE OF OF THE WORLD.

John 6:51

The first and by far the best and most important among all aids and means to purity is the reception of Christ in Holy Communion. There is no better means. Frequent, daily, devout communion is incomparably the best. Being united with the chaste body of Jesus Christ does something to us and for us which word cannot describe.

Every time this memorial sacrifice is offered up, the work of our redemption is carried on. We have Holy Communion, the fruit of the sacrifice in which He feeds us with His own "Body and Blood." He who eats my flesh and drinks my blood abides in me and I in Him.

At holy service, it is Christ in our midst that we confide in; we rejoice and sing aloud to Him. Remember too, that the time receiving Holy Communion is one of the most opportune moments for nurturing and invigorating the life of the soul, as Jesus in those moments becomes our spiritual food.

Yet, the life of the soul, when super-naturalized, is nurtured by God Himself, by His graces, His sacrament, by His Body and Blood given to us in Holy Communion. Such is the nourishment of our soul, such is the food which sustains and vivifies us. Now, super-naturalized by grace, their merit is so great, as to confer on us a legitimate right to aspire to the life of heaven.

We have an obligation to cooperate with the life of grace. To work with it, so that day by day this divine life may grow and develop within our souls. Our most urgent preoccupation should be to take care to preserve this life, and never to lose it, careful to rid ourselves of all dangers and temptations that might endanger it.

The suffering of Christ earned divine life for us—the memorial of His passion and death. In baptism we received divine life, but the Holy Communion preserves, develops it. Recall the Lord's own words: He who feeds on my flesh and drinks my blood has life eternal and I will raise him up on the last day. For my flesh are real food and my blood real drinks. Whoever eats my flesh and drinks my blood remains in me, and I in Him.

The Holy Communion prepares us to a happy future, for a blessed meeting with our returning Lord. It is our Light, our Shield, and our Citadel of Strength. Let us watch over it incessantly. He calls us constantly to draw nearer to Him.

— ♥ —

Dear Jesus, I thank You for Your love for me, especially for the Holy Communion. Your own personal gift of Yourself to me as food, it is for me, a traveler of my way to eternal home— the Food that will give me strength on my journey. May my Holy Communion reflect not only Your act of sacrifice, but also Your generosity. Though divine You came to me in order to change and transform me into Yourself. I must answer such generosity. I want each month, each hour, and each minute, to be Yours. Please help me my savior Jesus. Amen.

PRAY IN A SPIRIT OF THANKSGIVING

Colossians 4:2

Each and everything in life is an added reason to be thankful, even suffering and disappointments for all things are from God. He works in all things for our good, and bring long-term profit from them. Faith always strengthened right at the place of disappointment and suffering. We need to pause to recount His loving, providential care. How generous is God in bestowing His gift upon us, life, breath, health, family and friends. Every heart beat is a special blessing from God.

As we pray we must always remember His bounteous gifts to us. The Scriptures also remind us that God wants His children to thank Him. On numerous occasions Jesus taught us by His example as He turned to His Father in thanksgiving.

Since God is so good to us, it is obvious that we must respond in gratitude for all His blessings. God wants our prayers of thanksgiving. He wants us to come to Him with hearts filled with joy and gratitude.

Jesus taught us the importance of rendering thanks to the Father. He offered thanks before some of His miracles, before the multiplication of the loaves, before instituting the Lord's Suffer. He tells us that every Christian should have a heart "overflowing with gratitude" (Colossians 2: 7).

Furthermore, gratitude moves God's heart to shower His bounteous gifts more profusely upon us, for it is the way of God to enrich us with His abundant blessings and graces. Gratitude also generates in our soul, a more perfect reliance upon Divine Providence, as the soul realizes that God who is so liberal, will never leave a grateful heart.

A song of gratitude should be on our lips even in sufferings when we do not understand the ways of God, for we know that God's will is for our own good. Thankfulness is related to faithfulness.

Never forget that the nobility proper to a Christian demands a spirit of gratitude toward God and men. Life in Christ is not easy, rather a continuing struggle. Trust and confidence in God provides the "ultimate weapons."

Finally, gratitude begets sympathy and understanding in others. A grateful man is loved by all. There is nothing better than gratitude to gain the hearts of others.

Dear Jesus, I thank You for all the years that are gone and all the graces and blessings I received. There was joy and there was sorrow, but You were there too. I want to serve You always with a new song of thanks in my heart. Make me a good example to everyone I meet, the one who loves You and serves You is always happy. Yes, I thank You from my heart for all You have done for me. Just make me worthy of it all. Amen.

WHOEVER DIVORCES HIS WIFE AND MARRIES ANOTHER COMMITS ADULTERY AGAINST HER, AND THE WOMAN WHO DIVORCES HER HUSBAND AND MARRIES ANOTHER, COMMITS ADULTERY.

Mark 10:11-12

The Bible says: Husbands and wives must be faithful to each other. To the husband it says: Be happy with your wife and find your joy with the girl you married. Today many couples do not allow the counsel from God's word to help them work out their problems and they seek a divorce. Does God approve of divorce as a way to settle problems? No, He does not. He meant marriage to be a lifelong arrangement.

What if your marriage mate has refused to study God's word with you, or even opposes your Christian activities? The Bible still encourages you to stay with your mate and not to view separation as the easy way out of your problem. Do what you personally can, to improve the situation in your home—by applying what the Bible says in regard to your own conduct. In time, because of your Christian conduct you may win over your mate (1Corinthians 7:16). And what a blessing will be yours if your loving patience is rewarded in this way.

Even in families that are normally happy, from time to time there will be problems. This is because all of us are imperfect and do wrong things. We all stumble many times, says the Bible (James 3:2). A marriage mate should not demand perfection from each other. Therefore, neither mate should not expect a perfectly happy marriage, since; this is not possible for imperfect people to achieve.

Of course a husband and wife will want to work at avoiding what irritates the other mate. Yet, no matter how hard they try—at times they will upset the other. How difficulties can be handled? Difficulties can be handled in a powerful loving way. The Bible's counsel is: "Love covers a multitude of sins" (1 Peter 4:8). This means that mates who show love will not keep bringing up the mistakes the other has made. Love says in effect, yes, you made a mistake. But do I, at times. So I'll overlook yours and you may do the same for me.

When couples are willing to admit mistakes and try to correct them, many arguments and heartaches can be avoided. Their goal should be to solve problems, not to win arguments. Even if your mate is clearly wrong, make it easier to solve the problem by being kind. If you are at fault, humbly ask forgiveness. Do not postpone it, handle the problem without delay. You need to obey the Bible's command: Clothe yourself with tender affection of compassion, kindness, lowliness of mind, mildness, and long-suffering. But beside all these things, clothe yourselves with love for it is a perfect bond of union (Colossians 3:12-14).

With divine wisdom, the Bible says: "Husbands ought to love their wives as their own bodies" (Ephesians 5:28). This means that a husband should give his special attention, including tenderness, understanding and reassurance. He needs to assign her honor, as the Bible says, he does this by taking her into consideration in all that he does. In this way he will earn her respect (1Peter 3:7).

What about wives? The wife should respect her husband, the Bible declares, (Ephesians 5:33) the failure to heed this counsel is a chief reason why some husbands resent their wives. A wife shows respect by supporting her husband's decisions and by cooperating wholly with Him to achieve family goals. By fulfilling her assigned role as helper and complement to her husband, she make it easy for him to love her.

As the Bible says, the woman was made as a helper to her husband. In keeping with that role, the Bible urges: "Let wives be in subjection to their husband." (Ephesians 5:22).

A marriage or a family needs leadership. The man was created with greater measure of qualities, and strengths required providing such leadership. For this reason the Bible says: A husband is the head of his wife as Christ is the head of the church (Ephesians 5:23).

The love of a man for his wife is the love of surrender. For the completeness of this surrender, individual rights cede to mutual rights. According to the Apostle Paul in His first letter to the Corinthians, stresses the mutual obligation between husband and wife. "Let every man have His own wife, and let every woman have her own husband.

Christ restored the unity of marriage, which means that man can only have one wife and woman can only have one husband. They take each other for better or for worse, for richer for poorer, until death separates them. Christ teaching on this point is final: Whoever shall put away his wife, (not for fornication) and shall marry another commits adultery against her, and if a wife puts away her husband and marries another shall commit adultery (Mark 10:11-12). When a husband and wife have lived together in Christian marriage only after the death of the other party is free to remarry.

Marriage is a contract between one man and one woman to give themselves for life and become husband and wife. But Christian marriage is more than a contract, it has been elevated by Christ to a holy contract—it is sacrament.

Many family problems today involved children. What can be done if this is the case in your family? First of all, as parents you need to set a good example. This is because children are more inclined to follow what you do than what you say. And when your actions differ from your words, young ones are quick to see it. So, if you want your children to live fine Christian lives, you must set the example (Romans 2:21-22).

One of the most beautiful things upon earth is the family. God and nature have made it sacred; its members are bound together by Holy love.

—❤—

Dear Jesus, who by Your sublime and beautiful virtues of humility, patience, poverty, obedience, modesty, charity and gentleness—blessed with peace and happiness. Grant us the grace to love one another in mutual charity. Look upon us in Your loving kindness. Help us to obey You in all things, Lord, and give us strength to persevere till the end of our journey. Amen.

GOLD AND SILVER ARE TESTED BY FIRE, AND A PERSON'S HEART IS TESTED BY THE LORD.

Proverbs 17:3

Happy is the person who remains faithful during times of trials, because when he succeeds in passing such a test, he will receive as his reward the life which God has promised to those who love Him. According to James, "My brethren, count it pure joy when you are involved in all sorts of trials. Realize that when your faith is tested, this makes for endurance. Let endurance come to its perfection, so that you may be fully mature and lacking in nothing. But God keeps His promise, and He will not allow us to be tempted beyond our strength to endure it, and provides us with the way out. Therefore, let us turn to Him to make us sharers of His cross. Let us conform ourselves to His Holy adorable will, and earnestly call upon Him for His help, and protection.

We may lay down as a law of Divine Providence that each one of us will undergo temptations. It is necessary that temptation should try you. To serve God, prepare yourself for trials and temptations. "Blessed is the man who suffers temptation." Therefore, it is necessary that we should always be ready to resist and overcome them.

Christ our Lord, by presenting Him as a model which every man is bound to study and know, and to copy in His own life, in mind, heart, and behavior. To follow Christ is a great and glorious service. It is a real pathway to happiness. It is also a crown of glory to us hereafter in Heaven—that the suffering of this time are not worthy to be compared with the glory to come, that shall be revealed in us. Whoever does not take up his cross and follow in my steps is not fit to be my disciple (Matthew 10:38). If we suffer we shall also reign with Him.

We too, have pledged ourselves to follow Him in all this: Namely, to know Him more clearly, to study His poverty, obedience, humility, and opposition to the world, and we may love Him more dearly, and imitate Him more closely in these virtues.

God allows His servants to be tempted in order that He may fill them with humility, and render them mistrustful and different in their own strength, whilst at the same time it leads them closer to our Lord, and causes them to repose their confidence in His protection.

Another reason why God permits His servant to be tempted, in order that by His grace they may increase their merits here, and their glory hereafter. We must not suppose that we are making great progress in virtue when all goes smoothly.

Yes, trials are necessary, and they can at all time turn to our great profit and spiritual advantage, if we only employ the means that which God has provided us. The same truth insisted by the Apostle James: Blessed is the man that has been proved, he shall receive the crown of life.

Trials and temptations awaits those who enter into an earnest service of God, that far from being a mark of God's displeasure, they should be accepted rather as a sign of His approbation, and goodwill in our regard as being special proofs of His favor and love. It is a great glory, to follow the Lord!

Lastly, let us resolve to practice an exact obedience in the spirit of faith. True sanctity consists in accomplishing the will of God.

Dear Jesus, make me change my life. I acknowledge You, to be almighty God. I beg You to vanish all my proud thoughts, and my self-love that I may ever humble, and willingly embrace suffering, and contempt. Grant that I may now crucify all my evil desire, so that I may have happiness of living, and dying crucified with You, and in the end with the delight of heaven. Amen.

ASK, AND IT SHALL BE GIVEN TO YOU, SEEK AND YOU SHALL FIND, KNOCK AND IT SHALL BE OPENED TO YOU. FOR EVERYONE WHO ASKS RECEIVES, AND HE WHO SEEKS, FINDS, AND TO WHOM WHO KNOCKS IT SHALL BE OPENED.

Matthew 7:7

Prayer is a relationship with God. As we spend time in prayer, this relationship grows and become more intimate. Prayer is the key to the Father's heart. People of prayer are invincible people. They are not conquered by the evil one, by any resistance, by any suffering or difficulties in life. Prayer is the surest weapon for victory. People of prayer are always happy people.

Now, the most important question is: How are we using this most powerful gift which God has given us. "Ask and you shall receive..." Jesus is the master teacher. He taught us how to pray. He advices us to ask in His name: Whatever you ask the father in my name I will do (John 14:14). The important thing is we must ask in the right way. Only the right prayers are answered. This is basic biblical truth. God commits Himself to His word only when we ask in harmony with His will.

Jesus taught us to pray both by His instruction and also by His example. He encourages us to step out in faith and ask what is necessary for our salvation. Christ said: If you are ready to believe that you will receive whatever you ask for in prayer, it will be done for you. You will receive all that you pray for, provided you have faith (Matthew 21:22). This is important requisite for prayer.

To pray in the name of Jesus means that we must have the mind and heart of Jesus. In other words our prayer should be only what Jesus seeks or wants. Our thoughts, hopes, and desires should be perfectly in accord with the mind of Christ. When we cultivate this attitude, then we speak with the power and authority of Jesus. As the Apostle Paul teaches us, that our mentality must be that of Christ (Philippians 2:5). Again, he says: "Acquire a fresh spiritual way of thinking, you must put on a new man" (Ephesians 4:23). When our thinking is in tune with Jesus Christ, then, our prayer will be pleasing to God, and will be granted for His honor and glory.

Jesus taught us how to pray, "Thy will be done." We must not only accept God's will, but we must also have a great desire to do His will always, even if it leads us to the valley of suffering.

Obedience is a grant expression of our love of Jesus Christ, and of self surrender to Him. Obedience begets a generosity of love, which is the only habitual attitude toward God; because obedience unites us to God, and makes us participate habitually in His life through sanctifying grace. Obedience gives us great security for it guarantees the one condition of all perfection, the fulfillment of the will of God.

Prayer brings all spiritual exercises to bear upon it. Meditate on the obedience of Christ. Obedience is hard for any uninspired soul. So we must ask for grace and inspiration from Him.

Let us live our lives in God's hands. He is a loving Father and whatever He permits He will turn all things to our good. This attitude of trust in God is a genuine prayer.

In prayer, let us discern how wholeheartedly is our daily acceptance of Him in whatever manner He may come to us. In prayer let us captivate His mentality.

"Prayer changes things..."

Dear Jesus, I put my trust in You. Strengthen my faith, hope and love. Please help me not to separate myself from You my loving Redeemer. Make me ever walk in the path of Your precepts, following Your shinning example. Make me humble, patient, and obedient to Your will. Unite me so closely with You that I may be more like You. Fill my heart with great love for You! I beg You to hear my humble prayer, in Jesus name. Amen.

SEEK TRUE PEACE, NOT UPON EARTH, BUT IN HEAVEN, NOT IN MEN, NOR THINGS CREATED, BUT IN GOD ALONE.

John 14: 27

Peace of mind is extremely valuable treasure, and enables us to make progress in virtue. This provides us with strength, and courage under temptation, and difficulties. But without peace, we become inconsistent and fickle, despondent, and rebellious under trials.

A clear and strong conviction, that sufferings are the law of existence for all men, and much more for Christian. Therefore, the only wise course is that we should submit at least patiently.

If we once and for all determine to resign ourselves into the hands of God, we shall find by experience that He will fill us with happiness and peace, and all things will turn to our spiritual welfare. We are then under the care of a loving Father who is almighty, all wise, and all good. For we know that all things work together for good to them that love God.

Besides, we have the greatest gift we can enjoy— namely, the testimony of good conscience. To be able to see the truth—we serve God, we serve a good Master who loves us,

Mila Rayot

and whom we love; it is a real joy and makes the approach of death an actual pleasure to us.

Banish all anxiety about future troubles, which probably will never arise. And prepare yourself for what's ahead, with perfect resignation to the ever-blessed will of God.

Let your spiritual life be marked with prudence, courage, and consequently when you fall, don't yield to immoderate grief, but make an act of contrition and renew your fervor. Acknowledge your shortcomings, and conceive high purposes of virtue: But banish any desire of perfection which disturbs the peace of your soul.

Let us entreat His grace that our will be united to His Adorable will. "All who humble themselves before the Lord shall have wonderful peace."

I Love You Divine Jesus, my Lord and Master. Make strong and real my faith with the sublime, and beautiful virtues of humility, obedience, poverty, modesty, charity, patience, and gentleness, blessed with peace, and happiness. I beg You to enlighten me that I may be able to walk in Your holy light. Strengthen me with the grace of Your Holy Spirit, and give Your peace to my soul that I may be free from all needless worry and care. Your peace, which is the only true peace, so that by obeying Your commandments I may come at last to the glory of heaven. Amen.

WE STRUGGLE AND WORK HARD BECAUSE WE HAVE PLACED OUR HOPE IN THE LIVING GOD, WHO IS THE SAVIOR OF ALL AND ESPECIALLY OF THOSE WHO BELIEVE.

1Timothy 4:10

It is an act of justice to serve God. We come from Him, from Him alone, entirely from Him, always from Him. We can then if we really wish, learn once for all to overcome ourselves, and determine our manner of life, without allowing ourselves to be influenced by any affections which are not approved by the teachings of faith, and right reason.

In the first place, we are instructed how to banish from our hearts all evil affections, and having done this, we shall be in a better disposition to seek and to discover the will of God, concerning ourselves and all the circumstances of life. We shall be able to form such resolutions as God will show us to be pleasing to Him.

We must go through it with great generosity of hearts and without reserve, leaving ourselves in the hands of God to do with us as He pleases, ever ready to grant whatever He may ask, and make any sacrifice which He may call for.

We must have courage to face the difficulties which the devil will put in our way. God is with us, and through Him we shall conquer. If God is for us, who can be against us? (Romans 8:31). Again, when He walked the earth as man, He cried out: Come, all who labor and are burdened, and I will refresh you" (Matthew 11:28).

Our undertaking is a hard one, but our strength is our hope in God. The greater our hope, the more blessed shall we be, and the measure of His mercy will be according to our hope.

Jesus Christ works in His Mystical Body, Aiding, Enlightening, Interceding for us with His Father. He is the teacher of His people, to instruct them on the way to heaven, to conduct them all, whether ignorant or learned, poor or rich, weak or strong, toward their eternal home.

Let us then resolve to apply ourselves with all diligence to perform each of our duties. This diligence must be exercised in maintaining our knowledge of sacred learning.

Furthermore, it is necessary that we cut off all occasion of dissipation, and distraction as far as possible in our state of life—not a time for pleasure and amusement, but for laboring and sowing the seeds of virtue, which grow and ripen into the fruit of eternal life. It is necessary that we cultivate interior recollection and union with God, that we foster the spirit of devotion and that we prove faithful to our daily meditation and our other spiritual duties. Above everything, love one another earnestly, because love covers many sins. (1 Peter 4:8).

Above all, we must earnestly practice internal mortification, withdrawing our hearts from all worldly things that we may fix them in God alone.

Let us ask the Lord for special grace which we desire, that we should not be deaf to His call but prompt and diligent in fulfilling His most holy will. Let us earnestly pray to Jesus, who guides us and moves us to repentance and entire confidence in His mercy and love.

Dear Jesus, life is never easy and it gets real hard at times. I want to fight bravely all the time. Truly, You are my protector and helper. The only thing that holds me up is the consciousness that I can rely on Your grace, and that You will never fail me even in my darkest, heaviest hour. I need you always, so be near to me. Never let either joy or sorrow lessen my love for You in any way. Jesus, thank You for Your grace. I don't mind what happens to me now, if only You take me to heaven with You forever. Amen.

HE WHO HUMBLES HIMSELF SHALL BE EXALTED.

Luke 18:14

The spirit of the world is pride, and the spirit of Christ is humility. He humbled Himself, taking the form of a servant, and became obedient unto death, even to the death of the cross (Philippians2:7).

Christ was without sin, but for our sake God made Him share the righteousness of God (2 Corinthians 5:21). For though He is God, yet He humbled Himself, "Emptied Himself." And bids us to learn about Him because He is humble of heart. God is gentle, lovely, amiable, and full of sincerity and truth.

The whole life of our blessed Lord, from His Incarnation to His Death upon the cross, must convince us of the beauty, excellence, and necessity of this virtue. The cross teaches us the price paid for our souls. Knowing that we were not redeemed with corruptible things as gold and silver, but with the precious Blood of Christ, as of a lamb unspotted and undefiled. Therefore, the Son of God came down from heaven full of grace and truth, and assumed our human nature imparting to it an infinite price and dignity. "The word was made flesh, and dwelt amongst us," and was made in all things to us, except that He has no sin.

He has not only manifested this humility in His own person, but required that His disciples should imitate Him in practice of this virtue, when He said to them that they must be humble as children, if they wished to enter into the kingdom of Heaven.

The practical recognition is that, our absolute dependence is the most pleasing to God our Lord, who is the spirit of truth and therefore, we will find all good things and blessings promise to those who are truly humble.

Real happiness dwells only in the soul, and cannot be produced by riches, which are mostly external and material. What does real happiness consists? Innocence, love, joy—and of these neither sickness, misfortune, nor poverty can't rob it. How beautiful is the grace of innocence compared with any natural beauty—the beauty of soul when in the state of grace.

Let us learn a lesson of meekness and patience from our gentle Lord and master. Let our thoughts dwell upon the particular injuries and humiliations we most dread, and then fixing our eyes upon Jesus the model of patience. Let your patience show itself perfectly in what you do. Then you will be perfect and complete. You will have everything you need. But if any of you needs wisdom you should ask God for it. God is generous. He enjoys giving to all people, so God will give you wisdom (James 1:4-5).

Let us pursue justice, godliness, charity, and patience, encouraging each other in the practice of this virtue. It is necessary for us to practice patience, so that we can enjoy inner peace and merit an everlasting crown.

Living a victorious crucified life with Him, we will persevere to the end and die upon the cross. Let us contemplate our Lord as He hangs there in the midst of suffering. Truly, He is by excellence the Man of sorrows—for He suffers not one pain alone, but every variety of racking pains, together with the bitterest heartbreaking sorrow.

Therefore, let us take courage and firmly resolve to suffer much and labor hard for Him, in as much as we are sure, "if we suffer with Him, also we reign, and in proportion as we share in His labors, we shall also partake of His reward.

Let us look to Scriptures for light and render more and more perfect service to God in our ordinary lives, a glory which is real, constant, and eternal.

Lastly, prayer if properly made is the strength of our hearts: It enables us to ask and to wait with patience and hope, knowing that God's timing is perfect, and our petitions will be granted. "As the scripture says, He gives generously to the needy, His loving kindness lasts forever."

My dearest Jesus crucified! Who because of Your burning love for us willed to be crucified, and shed Your Precious Blood for the redemption and salvation of our soul. I thank You for the infinite love, with which You have endured such terrible sufferings. Destroy in me all pride and give me true humility, so that I can serve you faithfully with my whole heart, everyday of my life. Amen.

THE FRUIT OF THE SPIRIT IS LOVE, JOY, PEACE, PATIENCE, KINDNESS, GOODNESS, FAITHFULNESS, GENTLENESS, AND SELF-CONTROL

Galatians 5:22-23

The Spirit of God gives witness to our spirit that we are children of God. We are heirs of God and joint heirs with Christ; for if we suffer with Him, we shall also be glorified with Him.

If Christ is in us the body is dead to sin, while the spirit lives because of justice. The Lord reveals Himself to His people, with remarkable honesty. Through our Lord Jesus Christ, justice comes from everyone who believes. Justice that comes from faith, says the Lord.

Our thoughts should be wholly, directed to all that is true, all that deserve respect, all that is honest, pure, admirable, decent, virtuous, and become imitator of the Lord, receiving great trials with joy that comes from the Holy Spirit.

Follow the way of love, even as Christ loves us. We should avoid giving anyone offense, on contrary, in all what we do we strive to present ourselves as children of God. We are called by Jesus to love, and to live by God's commandments everyday.

God does not call us to live in immorality, but to holiness. Therefore, he who rejects this instruction rejects not man, but God who sends His Holy Spirit upon you (1Thessalonians 4:7-8). Because we are God's chosen ones, holy and beloved, clothe yourselves with heartfelt mercy, kindness, humility, meekness, and patience. But above all these virtues, put on love that binds the rest and makes us perfect.

Christ's peace must reign in our hearts, since as members of one body; we have been called to that peace. To be closely united in love, enriched with full assurance by the knowledge of the mystery of God: Namely Christ...in whom are hidden all the treasures of wisdom, and knowledge.

By the might of His glory, we will be endowed with strength needed to stand fast, even to endure joyfully whatever may come. Then, we will multiply good works of every sort and grow in the knowledge of God. The only way to live a good life is to live according to God's word.

Get rid of all bitterness, all passion and anger, harsh words, slander, and malice of every kind. In place of these, be kind to one another, compassionate, and mutually forgiving just as God has forgiven us in Christ (Ephesians 4:31).

We need to be patient with God's will, and receive what He has promised. Always seek one another's good, and for that matter the good of all. Our deepest desire is to show the same zeal till the end. Do not grow lazy but imitate those who through faith and patience are inheriting the promises. We are persuaded of better things in our regard, things pointing to our salvation. We are not among those who draw back and perish, but among those who have faith and live.

In summary, then, all of us should be like-minded, sympathetic, loving toward one another, kindly disposed, and humble. Do not return evil for evil, or insult for insult. Return a blessing instead. This we have been called to do, that we may receive a blessing as our inheritance. Those who have endured we call blessed. Today, if you hear His voice, harden not your hearts. (Hebrews 3:15).

God has saved us and has called us to a holy life. Take a model of sound teaching what we heard, in faith, hope, and love in Jesus Christ. What we are aiming for in this warning is the love that springs from a pure heart, and good conscience and sincere faith. Above all, let our love for one another be constant, for love covers a multitude of sins (1 Peter 4:8). Persevere in God's love, and welcome the mercy of our Lord Jesus Christ which leads us to life eternal.

It is necessary for us to live lives of temperance, as it is to regulate them by the exercise of prudence, justice, and fortitude. Let us not forget that everything which our Lord permits is intended for our good, either directly or indirectly, and consequently let us drink the chalice, for it is presented to us by our Father in Heaven. Be steadfast in it!

My loving Jesus, You know my weakness. I fail to do the good I wish, strengthen me by the power of the Holy Spirit. Make me O Lord, obedient without complaint, poor without regret, humble without pretense, patient without murmur, joyous without frivolity, and truthful without disguise. Bestow on me, O Lord, understanding to know You, diligence to seek You, a life which may please You, and a hope which may embrace You. Amen.

TAKE CARE TO DO ALL THESE THINGS, FOR YOU KNOW THE TIME IN WHICH WE ARE LIVING.

Romans 13:11

At the beginning perhaps we wasted our time without any conscious malice in a childlike manner. However, malice increased with age, for as we grow older we realized the grievousness of this loss, but we never made a definite change for the better. This will be the cause of the greatest torments of the damned in hell— consciousness of the time they lost so miserably, and with which they could have so easily accomplished their salvation.

Brethren, walk as the wise, redeeming time. Let us start now a life of new fervor, renewing our effort to employ all the time remaining to us in the service of God. According to the "Imitation of Christ," it is not precisely a long life which is agreeable in the eyes of God, but only a life that no matter how short it may have been, has been distinguished by the good use of time.

How many men and women at the end of their lives, anxiously long for one day more, even a few minutes more to atone for their sins? To gain some merits, so to be able to appear worthy in the presence of Almighty God? And yet how little we make use of the time so generously granted to us! It is an incredible folly to squander not merely a treasure, but a priceless mine, the source of treasure—our precious time.

Let us not forget that in the course of each passing hour, we are granted many new graces, and by wasting time a miserable contempt for them are implied. So the Bible says: "use your time well... guard yourself from evil, and bring upon yourself no shame." I tell you that every idle word that men speak, will give account in the Day of Judgment (Matthew 12:36).

The Holy Scriptures are full of warnings with respect to this point, the days of man are short, and they are filled with many miseries. Nay, it is short. It passes as a cloud over the face of heaven, or as the spring flowers of the field. By these and other comparisons does the spirit of God impress this truth upon us?

Our dear Lord in His parables urges this truth upon us, thereby to guard us against any waste of time, and impel us to employ it well. He declares that He will come like a thief in the night, when we least expect it.

Dear Jesus, heaven is at the end of the road of life, only if I keep on the right road. I now beg Your grace to be always eager to await Your call at the day of Your coming. So to live that whether You come in the evening, You will find me ready to come home to You. Then I shall be Yours always. Amen.

THE BEATITUDES

Matthew 5:3-11

HOW BLEST ARE THE POOR IN SPIRIT FOR THE REIGN OF GOD IS THEIRS. They are blessed, for they are the objects of the special love of Jesus Christ, they are in station more like His own, being shaped by the spirit of Christ, and to be fully dedicated to serving the true God, are on the right road to eternal beatitudes.

BLEST ARE THE SOROWING, THEY SHALL BE CONSOLED. This blessing is not given to all who mourn, it is bestowed only on those who in sorrow and resignation accept their trials, who bewail their own flesh and its concupiscence, and who are faithful in times of desolation. These shall be comforted in the next world by the enjoyment of the future glory which shall be revealed in them, and because in the present life also their love of God will make those things sweet to them in which human nature regards as sad and bitter.

BLEST ARE THEY WHO HUNGER AND THIRST FOR HOLINESS THEY SHALL HAVE THEIR FILL. They who hunger and thirst after habitual justice by which they are sanctified, and after actual justice by which they are perform, and ever strenuous in the exercise of virtue, aspire to that which is perfect, and strive to unite themselves more and more closely with our Lord by a lively faith, and ardent charity, and by frequent Holy communions. It is to these that are rich in abundance of supernatural gifts, and graces that are promised: And "He fills them with good things.

BLEST ARE THEY WHO SHOW MERCY, MERCY SHALL BE THEIRS.

That man is merciful or pitiful of heart that love and assists those who are wretched, whether they suffer externally or internally. But these mercies must rest on a supernatural basis, and exercised for God's sake if it is to secure the blessing. It is more blessed to give than to receive in the teaching of Jesus Christ. But the world reverses this divine saying, by its maxim that it is "Happier to get than to receive."

Our eternal lot is to be decided by our mercifulness, for it is by charity, that a multitude of their sins is covered. The merciful even in this life are led by God's grace, to seek remission of their sins and in the next life are made partakers of eternal mercy.

BLEST ARE THE SINGLE-HEARTED FOR THEY SHALL SEE GOD.

The clean heart, are those who are not conscious of unrepented sins which stain the soul. Seek only to please God in all things with special clearness of spirit which is life and peace. However, if we are single-hearted, we must love God with all our whole hearts.

BLEST ARE THE PEACEMAKERS, THEY SHALL BE CALLED SONS OF GOD.

This term indicates those who are meek, and show themselves amiable and gentle to all, who avoid giving offense to others unless it is in good course. Such too, are they who smooth down quarrels, reconcile persons at variance, and strive to implore men to seek reconciliation with God, and with Jesus Christ the Prince of Peace. These are called, and are in reality sons of God by adoption, and brothers of Jesus Christ through grace, and are most dear to Him who came down from heaven to establish this peace.

BLEST ARE YOU WHEN THEY INSULT YOU AND PERSECUTE AND UTTER EVERY KIND OF SLANDER AGAINST YOU BECAUSE OF ME.

To act bravely is to be a hero, but to suffer greatly and patiently is to be a Christian, seeing that to suffer is in general far harder than to do, whence we may say that of all Beatitudes this carries off the palm. To endure injuries, contempt, pain, and death because we observe the laws of God, this is full of merit. Such persecutions separate us from the world, and drive us to God. Be glad and rejoice! For your reward is great in heaven, they persecuted the prophets before you the very same way.

Blessed are the poor in spirit, the meek, they that mourn, they who hunger and thirst after justice, the merciful, the peacemakers, and they that suffer persecution.

For these lessons, relate to that perfect abnegation to which we where pledged to lay down our lives for the "Kingdom of Christ." Love calls us to lay down our lives in humble service as Jesus did to our sake. Just as the cross was the ultimate victory of our Lord—Christ Himself invites us to take up our cross and follow Him.

Let us consider their depth of meaning, the examples of each left for us by Jesus Christ and the reward attached to them. "Come ye to Him and be enlightened, and your faces shall not be confounded" (Psalm 34:5).

Christ says to us: You are the salt of the earth. But if the salt lose its savor wherewith shall be salted? (Matthew 5:13). You are the light of the world... so let your light shine before men, that they may see good your works, and glorify your father in heaven. (Matthew 5:16). If these two qualities are absent, we are fit for nothing.

In whatever state we may be, whether ecclesiastical or religious, whether in domestic life or holding authority, we are bound in due proportion to form ourselves according to the principle of the Beatitudes.

Let us implore to God to give us the grace to walk in the footsteps of our blessed Lord, especially by imitating His obedience, and humility, and by our fervor in performing the ordinary duties of our state of life. Let us beg earnestly to our dear Lord more intimately, we may love Him more ardently, we may listen to His call, and we may respond to it with greater devotion, and generosity.

Let us examine ourselves, and see how much we have been wanting in our efforts to secure the blessings that He promised. Let us make acts of sorrow for our past negligence, and strengthen them by adding firm resolution to strive more earnestly for the future.

— ❤ —

Dear Jesus, help me to do what You teach me, to be kind, humble, and pure. Grant that I may always desire what is most acceptable, and dear to You. Help me to live a good life dearest Jesus. Let me walk in obedience, self-denial, and sacrifice, which leads me to greater faith, and righteousness. Make me keep Your Beatitudes, and to do Your will always forever and ever. Amen.

TAKE THE HELMET OF SALVATION AND THE SWORD OF THE SPIRIT, WHICH IS THE WORD OF GOD.

Ephesians 6:17

Life in the service of God is not a time for play, it is indeed a time of real and solid happiness, but it is full of seriousness of suffering, and sacrifice. Nor can we wonder, for He Himself tells us, He loves each one of us with an everlasting love. He bought us with an infinite price with His most Precious Blood, and called us that hereafter we may share with Him in His glory for all eternity.

Our only boast must be that we are followers of crucified Christ, and to fulfill the will of God in regard to our life and conduct. We must imitate Jesus Christ, if we want to acquire an abundant life. Let us not be surprised at our temptations, Christ allowed Himself to be tempted to vanity, then to vainglory, and lastly to avarice! If we are acceptable to God, it is necessary that temptation should try us, for our benefits. God wishes to strengthen our faith. He wants to perfect us. Let us however fear nothing, but treat the devil with cool contempt that he will flee from us. God will give us the victory through our Lord Jesus Christ.

We must fear nothing, through Jesus Christ we shall overcome. And every act of resistance, every call upon Divine help will merit for us a crown of glory in Heaven. He wishes to illuminate us all, with the light of the truth.

Let us cheerfully cast ourselves at His sacred feet, and earnestly entreat Him to excite our hearts, to seek the highest perfection and entire detachment from all earthly things. He has "created" us in Christ by making us one in His Mystical Body—and there in, we are given sanctifying grace—countless actual graces with each special graces and help. We are bound to thank God always, because we are the fruits of those to whom God has chosen for salvation.

We are not to spend what remains of our earthly life on human desire, but by the will of God. We must not grow weary of doing what is right. Communion with God must be a true sincere desire and wish of our hearts.

Through Him we gained access by faith to the grace in which we now stand, and we boast of our hope for the glory of God. But not only that, we even boast of our afflictions! We know that affliction makes for endurance, and endurance for tested virtue, and tested virtue for hope.

Our Lord Jesus Christ set an example for us, so that we will do just what He has done for us. Remember the Lord in everything we do, and He will show us the right way. Let us humbly place ourselves in the presence of our Lord, as He guides and rules all things by His Divine Providence.

— ❤ —

Dear Jesus, I trust in You, because You know my needs. Make me seek Your truth always, truth in my words, my judgments, and my actions. Help me to think of others more than of myself, and to take care of them according to Your law and commandments, so that I may rejoice in Your freedom and salvation. Amen.

TRUST IN THE LORD WITH ALL YOUR HEART, NEVER RELY ON WHAT YOU THINK YOU KNOW.

Proverbs 3:5

Christian must have full confidence in Jesus. To seek salvation through observance of the law is not the source of justification. It is associated with justification only if it is observed through faith. The value of the law lay in its role of leading to an understanding of the absolute necessity of faith in Christ.

The Scriptures are the source of all wisdom, and loving fulfillment of God's word revealed in Christ, through whom man finds salvation. Christian life is to be inspired not only by the Old Testament men of faith, but above all by Jesus. As the architect of Christian faith, He endured the cross before receiving the glory of His triumph. Reflection on His sufferings, should give His followers courage to continue struggles if necessary, even to the shedding of blood.

To sustain trials, to achieve endurance and perfection, requires wisdom which God readily grants to believing petitioners, but withholds from those who doubt. A living faith works through love, as opposed to a dead faith that lacks good works. Every moment we must live in complete dependence on God. Trust includes full acceptance of the promises of God and unconditional commitment to His holy will.

The freedom of the Christian is that which is derived from the right order, i.e. service of God and reverence toward Him. Willingness to suffer with Christ equips the Christian with power to conquer sin... calmness, prayer, and constant love for one another through unfeigned hospitality, and generous use of one's gifts for the glory of Christ.

The gradation of testing endurance, and perfection, indicates the manner of achieving spiritual maturity, and full preparedness for the coming of Christ. The proper dispositions are submission to God, repentance, humility, and resistance to evil.

The qualities of the wise men endowed from above: innocence, peace, docility, sincerity, impartiality, sympathy, and kindly deeds: All contrast to earth bound wisdom with its cunning, jealousy, strife, inconstant, arrogance, and endless variety of vile behavior.

Continue with the theme of the transitory character of life on earth, traces impending ruin of the godless. It denounces the unjust rich, whose victims cry to heaven for judgment of their exploiters, the decay and corrosion of the costly garments and metals which here signalize wealth, prove them worthless and portend the destruction of their possessors.

Those oppressed by the unjust rich, are reminded of the need for patience, both in bearing the sufferings of human life and in their expectation in the coming of the Lord. It is then that they will receive their reward. As God invites the unjust to respond to Him through the evidence of His love, so the disciples of Jesus must be the bearers of the same love toward their enemies.

To be of great value before the eyes of the Lord, religious duties, public and private, must be performed for the single-hearted purpose of serving God and not for human esteem. God's unconditional love is His precious gift, which gives value to His sacrifices, was offered as evidence of the law of God. To function with a sense of personal responsibility for divine gifts received, and to be constantly aware of the primary love of neighbor.

The watchword is perseverance in a good cause, and trust in God's faithfulness and fidelity. Perseverance in the Christians vocation is the best preventative against losing it, and the safest provision for attaining its goal, entrance into the everlasting kingdom.

To avoid the danger of error and loss of security, the faithful are exhorted to persevere in the principles of the Christian life through growth in the knowledge of Christ. God is to be trusted, the God who called us to have fellowship with His Son Jesus Christ our Lord.

My dearest Jesus, at the same time I beg You, O Jesus, to enlighten me that I may be able to walk in Your holy light. I am nothing without Your guidance and help. Speak to my Soul, O Lord and command me to listen to Your voice. Enlighten my will to put Your words into practice, for You are my salvation, my life, and my peace, in time and eternity. Amen.

OUR ATTITUDE MUST BE
THAT OF CHRIST.

Philippians 2:5

The result which we draw from this is the conviction that the only true happiness of man, is to be found in the service of God during this life, by which we shall secure also eternal possession of Him hereafter. This service to God our Lord consists in the imitation of Christ, who assumed our nature in order to re-establish His Father's kingdom. We are called to follow Him in the "Kingdom of Christ."

Love means sacrifice. Christ our Lord in the heroic virtue, He choose hardship and injuries rather than pleasure. We learn to serve God and earnestly desire to reform and regulate our lives. The supreme happiness of life is the conviction that happiness is found in God alone. If we want to be raised with Christ, we must seek the things that are above... The conclusion will be, that the only happiness of man is to imitate Christ here, in the assured hope of rising with Him later, possessing Him eternally and of enjoying the happiness of loving our God, who is infinitely good to us.

What we should desire and consequently ask for is that, God would grant us light to see His Holy truth. On the teaching of truth, we are advised to imitate His life.

Wherefore, the soul must by humility and purity of heart, dispose itself to receive abundant grace, rather than on its own effort and industry to obtain it.

Christ our Lord by presenting Him as the model which every man is bound to study and to know and to copy His own life, in mind, heart, and behavior, whether this follows the extra-ordinary course, or beset with extra-ordinary difficulties and trials, such as our Lord underwent in His sacred passion and death.

In all our intentions, actions and endeavors, we must strive incessantly to be more devoted purely to the greater glory of God and to our soul salvation. This leads us into a close union with our Lord, in mind, heart, and will. It is great glory to follow the Lord. We absolutely required the help of God, which can be only secured by prayer.

In order that we may know ourselves thoroughly, we must examine and discover our evil inclinations, and be determined to subdue them. Such an aim as this is at once— solid, practical, easy, safe, and not liable to delusion. It is thus, that we are stimulated to carry out our holy resolutions and persevere with them until death.

We place His Divine Majesty and give honor to His well-beloved Son. Such motives were enough to make us firmly resolve to imitate Him to the best of our ability in the exercise of poverty, humility, and self-denial. At the same time the knowledge of the interior life which our true and Divine Leader invites us, along with the grace to follow in His footsteps and embrace His principles. In practice of spiritual poverty provided—that we can endure the sufferings and humiliations of it, without any sin or offense to God. This marks great progress in our attachment to the cause of our Lord and higher degree of perfection.

Let us then, from henceforth, place Jesus before our minds as our Master, Our Teacher, and our Model and let us resolve to lead a life in true conformity of His maxims. It's the only sure way to please God, to promote His glory and sanctify our own souls.

We beg for help and grace to know ourselves and to see ourselves as God sees us. We need to examine ourselves, in our thoughts, words, and actions. We should also recall the omissions of duty which we have been guilty of, as well as squandering valuable times or graces received. Let us walk with God, to be tune with His Spirit. He wants to give us the desires of our hearts.

Good Jesus, come and give me light to my mind and strength to my will. Fill my heart with great love for You. Unite me so closely with You that I may be more like You. I want to do Your will with love and obedience. I humbly offer You my needs and prayers of all the people I love. I thank You Jesus, for Your holy words. Help me to do what You teach me. Amen.

REMEMBER, SCRIPTURE SAYS, "BE HOLY FOR I AM HOLY"

1 Peter 1:16

Jesus is the Infinite Wisdom, given to the world as our Master, to teach us a new and heavenly doctrine. Jesus did say; to live according to the Holy Scriptures, if we want to enter into the kingdom of God. He is the way, the truth, and the life. Faith works by love—the love of enemies is the love that God shows to all. God is kind, compassionate, forgiving, and abundant in love. Paul urges us, I beseech you therefore, brethren, by the mercies of God, to present your bodies a living sacrifice, holy, and acceptable to God; which is your reasonable service.

Wherefore, the law of God is our school master to bring us unto Christ that we might be justified by faith. Through all our days, keep the Lord in mind and suppress every desire to sin or to break His commandments. Perform good works all the days of our life, and not to trade the path of wrongdoing—for if we are steadfast in our service, our good work will bring success.

Let us studiously avoid allowing ourselves, to speak or act solely according to the prompting and the dictates of our natural feelings. In the spirit of simple unquestioning faith, relying entirely on the loving providence of God, and let us assure ourselves that in the strength of our faith, we too shall conquer. The Apostle Paul says, "I can do all things through Christ who strengthens me." The Scriptures say: "Nothing is impossible with God."

If we are the instruments for the promotion of God's glory, we also must expect contempt and contradictions from the world. But trust in the Lord forever! For the Lord is an eternal Rock. He is the true light, which enlightens every man who comes into the world. But man prefers to remain in darkness. Let us commit ourselves to God and pray that He may shed the full blaze of His light on us, and may we abide within that blessed light.

Dear Jesus, I desire nothing except the perfect fulfillment in me of Your adorable will. Make me perfect in charity Lord, so that I may become blameless in Your sight. Give me all the graces necessary to serve You faithfully. I want to stand strong in your truth. Thank You for Your abundant love, and the opportunity to serve You. Help me to serve others as well, especially to those who are in need materially and spiritually, without expecting in return, reward or praise, but for Your honor and glory. Amen.

BLEST ARE YOU, WHOSE INIQUITIES ARE FORGIVEN AND WHOSE SINS ARE COVERED OVER.

Romans 4:7

Jesus told us: I am the resurrection and the life. Whoever believes in me, though he should die will come to life, and whoever believes in me will never die. If we died in Christ, we believe that we shall also live with Him. If we have united with Him through likeness to His death, so shall be through a life of resurrection.

We have now been justified by His blood, it is certain that we shall be saved by Him from God's wrath. For the sake of His own great name the Lord will not abandon His people. It is precisely that God proves His love for us: that while we were yet sinners, Christ died for us (Romans 5:8).

Unbelief and immorality has taken from life all purpose and happiness. Man had become the slaves of a reprobate sense, filled with all iniquity, malice, impurity, avarice, envy, murder, contentions, and deceit, blinded by pride, they are haughty, foolish, dissolute, disobedient to parents, and without mercy. Let us continue to sin that grace may abound? Certainly not! How can we die to sin and go on living in it?

Through disobedience we shall become sinners, so through obedience we shall become righteous.

Yes, affliction and anguish come upon every man who does evil. But there will be glory, honor and peace for everyone who has done good. With God there is no favoritism. In order that He will not have to punish us more severely later, we must make our ways straight before the Lord. God will reward or punish every person for what they have done. He will give eternal life to those who persist in doing what is good; God will give life forever to them. But other people are selfish and refuse to follow the truth. They follow evil. God will punish those who do not obey Him.

Do not therefore, let sin rule our mortal body and make us obey its lust, rather offer ourselves to God as men who have come back from the dead to life, and our bodies to God as weapon for justice. If we wish with our whole heart to return to God, put away our evil inclinations, devote ourselves to the Lord, and worship Him alone. Do not turn to meaningless idols which can never profit or save, they are nothing. If we continue to do evil we shall perish: For the wage of sin is death, but the gift of God is eternal life in Christ Jesus (Romans 6:23). That is why Christ died and came to life, that He might be the Lord of both the dead and the living. If we fear the Lord and worship Him and do not rebel against the Lord's commands, we follow the Lord our God. Keep in mind the great things He has done among us.

The righteousness of God revealed in the gospel, which begins and ends with faith. We must trust God, that He will soon have mercy on us and gather us together from everywhere, under the heavens to His holy place, for He has rescued us from great perils. The Lord watches over the way of the righteous.

If we believe in Him who raised Jesus from the dead, who has handle over death for our sins and rose up for our justification—in hope we were saved. And hoping for what we cannot see—means waiting with patience until the coming of our great God and savior Jesus Christ.

Be careful therefore, our Lord commanded us not turn aside to the right or to the left, but following exactly the way prescribed for us by the Lord, which we may live and prosper and may have a long life.

What God expects of us in relation to each other. Mainly, Love. If we focus on God's love and live out the ethical and moral content that defines love, we make God's eternal word beneficial to us.

But we need to see God who not only loves, but also cares desperately how people live. God has promised His guidance for the task—guidance through supernatural prompting, as we daily yield our will to Him—guidance through the principles in His words.

Dear Jesus, I pray You govern and sanctify my heart and body, my words and works, according to Your law and commandments. I beg Your mercy to forgive whatever sins I may have committed. In Your mercy and loving kindness receive my prayer, O Lord; cleanse my heart, so that no evil may have power over me. Be my ever present shield and my help. Amen.

YES, GOD SO LOVED THE WORLD THAT HE GAVE HIS ONLY SON, THAT WHOSOEVER BELIEVES IN HIM SHOULD NOT PERISH BUT HAVE ETERNAL LIFE.

John 3: 16

The greatest proof of God's love for men is the gift of His Son. Therefore, the one who loves shows that He is begotten of God, for God is love. The revelation of God consists in sending the Son of His love into the world, as our savior so that we might have life through Him.

Love consists in this: Not that we have loved God, but that He has loved us. Man has not merited God's love. It has been given freely and its value consists in sharing and continuing that love which is in God. He has sent His Son as an offering for our sins. An act of His mercy manifested through the death of Christ. This is the motive of our love for one another.

Through love for one another we can be certain that God dwells in us, and brings His love to perfection in us. Thus we are able to "see" and to know the invisible God. The proof of love for God consists in keeping His commandments. But the greatest of these is love of God and love of fellowmen—those begotten of God. Practical faith in this kind, confers a power that conquers the world of evil, as Christ overcome the world (John 16:33).

By accepting Christ as Son of God through faith, we receive Christ Himself who becomes in us the source of eternal life. Acceptance of the original light, gives promise of more in the future. Conversely, rejection of that light results in greater obscurity and misunderstanding.

As the glory of Christ's resurrection was preceded by His sufferings and death, the new life of faith which was bestowed will be subjected to many trials, while achieving its goal: The glory of the fullness of salvation at the coming of Christ.

Christ shows us generous patience: The longsuffering of Christ is a sign of His mercy toward man, who is slow to change. He is consumed by His love for us, suffered a terrible death upon the cross for our redemption, that He might teach us the way to heaven. Jesus is the only way to God.

Note the climatic gradation of qualities, beginning with faith and leading to the fullness of Christian life which is love. Fraternal love will overcome such evils that occur...and show humility toward one another, and complete trust in God's love. God wants all men to be saved and come to the knowledge of the truth. God can only save someone, if that someone makes the right choice. He wants all men to repent and obtained the forgiveness of sins by the grace of God.

Ask for the grace of an intimate knowledge of Jesus Christ, He is close to you; He is in you, His love is so great that we are called God's children (1John 3:1). Let us repent heartily and

116

resolve constantly, to act more wisely for the future. God is a generous loving God. He is God of power. He is God of hope and compassion.

Heavenly Father, I desire to serve You, to please You, to obey You, and to love You always. Give me a mind to know You, a will to serve You. Fill my heart that all my intentions and actions may be pleasing to You. I praise You, I thank You, and I love You, in union with Your dear Son Jesus Christ. May I be able to live always according to Your divine good pleasure, to do Your most holy will in all things, with a generous and willing heart and to persevere to love You till the end of my life. Amen.

KINDNESS IS LOVE IN ACTION

Dear Beloved Brothers and Sisters in Christ,

May God the Father and our Lord Jesus Christ grant you peace, love, and faith in great measure!

The most important and lasting gifts are those that are given from the heart. Among those things are honesty, openness, respect, kindness, compassion, genuine interest, and consideration.

Love is not a technique, it is a genuine art. Love creates an atmosphere of compassion, understanding and trust. Life becomes more beautiful and joyful each moment.

Love comes not to those who are merely good looking or talented—beauty and talent can never make a lasting relationship. What we can offer is a deep and everlasting love that money cannot buy. No amount of material wealth or fame could ever equal, the love between two people can have for each other.

Many people want to love each other, but find fault with each other. In the real world the amazing thing is that, it takes more energy to fight than to get along. A peaceful life allows a person to devote more energy to doing things he or she enjoys. We all seek happiness, but it only comes to those who work at it, and allow it to happen.

The best relationship is built up like a fine lacquer finish, with accumulated layers of kindness. It demonstrates that you have not taken your beloved for granted. You took the time to think what might bring a moment of happiness.

I have learned to value love. I have leaned to appreciate the importance of finding the right person, so that a marriage will last as long as the promises we make when we take the vow of "until death do us part." But what is certain is that love must last. The greatest is unselfish love. "Love never fails."

I believe that the promises made in marriage are serious and should last a lifetime. It is meant to be a lifelong arrangement, and it needs daily nurturing in order to have a strong foundation.

A happy marriage makes the world shine in a beautiful color. It makes you anxious to come home to each other to share and to care. Two hearts melt together in love, and understanding, which brings faithfulness and happiness. But if the marriage is wrong, the clouds cover any chances of happiness and everything about life is filled with sadness.

I never met anyone who disagreed with the axiom that love is the greatest thing in the world. But I frequently talk to people who despair of ever finding it; they are convinced that they are unlovable.

To be loved we must be lovable. For real love means action and service. Life is more beautiful when it is shared with love, which is unconditional, and asks nothing in return. That is the best love of all!

With Outmost Sincerity and Love,
Mila Rayot

GOD'S PROMISES

My Memory Verses for My Life

For God so loved the world that He gave His only Son, so that everyone who believes in Him will not perish but have eternal life.

John 3: 16 (NLT)

"But God showed His great love for us by sending Christ to die for us while we were still sinners."

Romans 5:8 (NLT)

I came that they have might life, and have it abundantly.

John 10:11 (NLT)

So whoever has God's Son has life; whoever does not have His Son does not have life.

1John 5:12 (NLT)

All men have sinned and are deprived of the glory of God.

Romans 3:23

If we say we have no sin, we are only fooling ourselves and refusing to accept the truth. But if we confess our sins to Him, He is faithful and just to forgive us and to cleanse us from every wrong.

1 John 1:8-9 (NLT)

"Jesus declared, I tell you the truth, unless a man is born again, he cannot see the Kingdom of God."

John 3:3

"Behold, I stand at the door and knock, if anyone hears my voice and opens the door, I will come in to him."

Revelation 3:20 (NLT)

"If anyone acknowledges me publicly here on earth, I will openly acknowledge that person before my Father in heaven. But if anyone denies me here on earth, I will deny that person before my Father in heaven."

Matthew 10:32 (NLT)

"Today, if you should hear His voice, harden not your hearts."

Hebrews 4:7

Whoever believes in God's Son have eternal life. Those who don't obey the Son will never experience eternal life, but the wrath of God remains upon them.

John 3:36 (NLT)

If we say, we are free of the guilt of sin, we deceive ourselves, and the truth is not to be found in us.

1 John 1:8

But if we acknowledge our sins He who is just can be trusted to forgive our sins and cleanse us from every wrong.

1John 1:9

Come now, let us set thing right, says the Lord. Though your sins like scarlet, they may become white as snow, though they be crimson red, they may become white as wool.

Isaiah 1:18-19

The wages of sin is death, but the gift of God is eternal life in Christ Jesus.

Romans 6:23 (NLT)

If declare with your lips, "Jesus is Lord" and believe in your heart that God raised Him from the dead, you will be saved. For we believe in one hearts and are put right with God, we declare with our lips and are saved.

Romans 10: 9-10

God saved you by His favor when you believed. And you can't take credit for this; it is a gift from God.

Ephesians 2:8

Through Him we have redemption, the forgiveness of our sins.

Colossians 1:14 (NLT)

For He has rescued us from the one who rules us in the kingdom of darkness, and He has brought us into the kingdom of His dear Son.

Colossians 1:13-14 (NLT)

Jesus said: I am the way, the truth, and the life. No one can come to the Father but through me.

John 14:6

Jesus said to all: Whoever wishes to be my follower: must deny his very self, take up his each day and follow in my steps.

Luke 9:23

Yes I am the vine; you are branches. Those who remain in me, and I in them, will produce much fruit. For apart from me you can do nothing.

John 15:5 (NLT)

Anyone who did accept Him he empowered to become a child of God.

John 1:12

Now turn from your sins and turn to God, so you can be cleansed of your sins.

Acts 3:19 (NLT)

Teach me how to live, O Lord. Lead me along the path of honesty.

Psalm 27:11 (NLT)

He saved us, not because of the good things we did, but because of His mercy.

Titus: 3:5 (NLT)

For the Lord your God is gracious and merciful. If you return to Him, He will not turn His face from you.

2 Chronicles 30:9 (NLT)

I myself no longer live, but Christ lives in me. So I live my life in this earthly body by trusting in the Son of God, who loved me and give Himself to me.

Galatians 2:20 (NLT)

It is impossible to please God without faith. Anyone who wants to come to Him must believe that there is a God and that He rewards those who sincerely seek Him.

Hebrews 11:6 (NLT)

For anyone who calls on the name of the Lord will be saved.

Romans 10:13 (NLT)

Search me, O lord, and know my heart; test me and know my thoughts. Point out anything in me that offends you and lead me along the path of everlasting life.

Psalm 139-23-24 (NLT)

The eyes of the Lord watch over those who do right, and His face against those who do evil.

1 Peter 3:12 (NLT)

The eye is the lamp of your body. When your eyesight is sound, your whole body is lighted up, but when your eyesight is bad, your body is in darkness. If your whole body is full of light and not partly in darkness, it will be as fully illumine as when a lamp shines brightly for you.

Luke 11:34-36

For though your hearts were full of darkness, now you are full of light from the Lord, and your behavior should show it! For this light within you produces only what is good and right and true.

Ephesians 5:8-9 (NLT)

I have come to the world as its light, to keep anyone who believes in me from remaining in the dark.

John 12:46

While you have light keep faith in the light, thus you will become sons of light.

John 12:36

In the same way, your light must shine before men so that they may see goodness in your acts and give praise to your heavenly Father.

Matthew 5:16

Here then, is the message we have heard from Him and announce to you, that God is light, in Him there is no darkness.

1 John 1:5

What this means is that if anyone is in Christ, he is a new creation. The old order has passed away, now all is new!

2 Corinthians 5:17

Therefore, as God's chosen people holy and beloved, clothes ourselves with compassion, kindness, humility, gentleness and patience. Bear with each other and forgive whatever grievance you may have against one another. Forgive as the Lord forgives you.

Colossians 3:12-13

And now you also have heard the truth, the Good News is that God saves you. And when you believed in Christ, He identified you as His own by giving you the Holy Spirit, whom He promised.

Ephesians 1:13-14 (NLT)

But grow in the special favor and knowledge of our Lord and Savior Jesus Christ.

2 Peter 3:18 (NLT)

Let your roots grow down into Him and draw up nourishment from Him, so you will grow in Faith, strong and vigorous in the truth you were taught.

Colossians 2:7 (NLT)

And remember, it is a message to obey, not just to listen to. If you don't obey, you are only fooling yourself.

James 1:22 (NLT)

Restore to me again the joy of your salvation, and make me willing to obey you.

Psalm 51:12 (NLT)

Obedience is far better than sacrifice.

1 Samuel 15:22 (NLT)

I have hidden your word in my heart that I might not sin against you.

Psalm 119:11 (NLT)

But for me, I will sing about your power. I will shout with joy each morning because of your unfailing love.

Psalm 59:16 (NLT)

For God has not given us a spirit of fear and timidity, but of power, love, and self-discipline.

2 Timothy 1:7

Worship the Lord with gladness.

Psalm 100:2 (NLT)

For I know the plans I have for you says the Lord. They are plans for Good and not for disaster, to give you future and hope.

Jeremiah 29:11 (NLT)

Commit everything you do to the Lord, and trust Him and He will help you.

Psalm 37:5 (NLT)

But blessed are those who trust in the Lord and made the Lord their hope and confidence.

Jeremiah 17:7 (NLT)

Jesus said: "Follow Me."

John 21:19

I have given you the example to follow. Do as I have done to you.

John 13:15 (NLT)

Follow God's example in everything you do, because you are His dear children. Live a life filled with love for others, following the example of Christ, who loved you and gave Himself as a sacrifice to take away your sins.

Ephesians 5:1-2 (NLT)

Anyone who wants to come to Him must believe that there is God and that He rewards those who sincerely seek Him.

Hebrews 11:6 (NLT)

Let the entire world look for me for salvation! For I am God; there is no other.

Isaiah 45:22 (NLT)

Trust the Lord with all your heart; do not depend on your own understanding. Seek His will in all you do, and He will direct your paths.

Proverbs 3:6 (NLT)

God is our protection and our strength. He always helps in times of trouble.

Psalm 45:1 (NLT)

Our help is from the Lord who made the heavens and the earth.

Psalm 124:8 (NLT)

I assure you until heaven and earth pass away, not the smallest letter of the law, not the smallest part of the letter, shall pass away until it all comes true. That is why whoever breaks the least significant of these commands and teaches others to do so shall be called least in the kingdom of God. Whoever fulfill and teaches these commands shall be great in the kingdom of God.

Matthew 5:18-20

"All mankind is like grass, and all their glory like the flower of the field. The grass withers, the flowers wilts, when the breath of the Lord blows upon it. So then, the people are the grass. Though the grass withers and the flowers wilts, the word of the Lord stand forever."

Isaiah 40:6-8

Don't copy the behavior and customs of this world, but let God transform you into a new person by changing the way you think. Then you will know what God wants you to do and you will know how good and pleasing and perfect His will really is.

Romans 12:2 (NLT)

The unfailing love of the Lord never ends! By His mercies we have been kept from complete destruction. Great is His faithfulness, His mercies begin afresh each day.

Lamentation 3:22-23 (NLT)

Such love has no fear because perfect love expels all fear.

1 John 4:18 (NLT)

And we know that God causes everything to work together for the good of those who love God.

Romans 8:28 (NLT)

The eyes of the Lord search the whole earth in order to strengthen those whose hearts are fully committed to Him.

2 Chronicles 16:9 (NLT)

Be still and know that I am God.

Psalm 46:10 (NLT)

No test has been sent you that does not come to all men. Besides, God keep His promise. He will not let you be tempted beyond your strength. Along with the test He will give you a way out of it so that you may be able to endure it.

1 Corinthians 6:17

Even though I walk through the dark valley of death, I will not be afraid, for you are close beside me. Your rod and your staff protect and comfort me.

Psalm 23:4 (NLT)

He gives power to those who are tired and worn out; He offers strength to the weak.

Isaiah 40:29 (NLT)

For our present troubles are quite small and won't last very long. Yet they produce for us an immeasurably great glory that will last forever!

2 Corinthians 4:17 (NLT)

We can rejoice, too, when we run, into problems and trials, for we know that they are good for us-they help us learn to endure. And endurance develops strength of character in us, and character strengthens our confident expectation of salvation. And this expectation will not disappoint us. For we know how dearly God loves us, because He has given us the Holy Spirit to fill our hearts with His love.

Romans 5:3-5 (NLT)

Wait patiently for the Lord. Be brave and courageous. Yes wait patiently for the Lord.

Psalm 27:14 (NLT)

But you must not forget, dear friends, that a day for the Lord is like a thousand years to the Lord, and a thousand years is like a day. The Lord isn't really being slow about His promise to return, as some people think. No, He is being patient for your sake.

2 Peter 3:8-9 (NLT)

For the Lord your God is going with you! He will fight for your enemies, and He will give you victory.

Deuteronomy 20:4 (NLT)

For I live in eager expectation and hope that I will never do anything that causes me shame, but that I will be bold for Christ, as I have been in the past, and that my life will always honor Christ, whether I live or die. For to me, living in Christ and dying is even better.

Philippians 1:20-21 (NLT)

And I am sure that God, who began the good work within you, will continue His work until it is finally finished on that day when Christ Jesus comes back again.

Philippians 1:6 (NLT)

See how very much our heavenly Father loves us, for He allows us to be called His children, and we really are! But the people who belong to this world don't know God, so they don't understand that we are His children.

1 John 3:1-2 (NLT)

Let us keep our eyes fixed on Jesus, who inspires and perfect our faith.

Hebrews 12: 2 (NLT)

If you want a happy life and good days, keep your tongue from speaking evil, and keep your lips from telling lies.

1 Peter 3:10 (NLT)

My brothers and sisters, take note of this: Everyone should be quick to listen, slow to speak and slow to get angry. Your anger can never make things right in God's sight.

James 1:19-20 (NLT)

If you live according to my teaching, you are truly my disciples, then you will know the truth, and the truth will set you free.

John 8:31-32

Most important of all, continue to show deep love for each other, for love covers a multitude of sins.

1 Peter 4:8 (NLT)

So do not fear, for I am with you; do not be dismayed for I am your God. I will strengthen and help you; I will uphold you with my righteous right hand.

Isaiah 41:10

Be still in the presence of the Lord, and wait patiently for Him to act.

Psalm 37:7 (NLT)

Don't worry about anything; instead, pray about everything. Tell God what you need, and thank Him for all He has done.

Philippians 4:6 (NLT)

A cheerful heart is good medicine, but a broken spirit saps a person's strength.

Proverbs 17:22 (NLT)

Always be full of joy in the Lord. I say it again rejoice!

Philippians 4:4 (NLT)

This is the day that the Lord has made. We will rejoice and be glad in it.

Psalm 118:24 (NLT)

Rejoice in the Lord always! I say it again rejoice! The Lord is near. Dismiss all anxiety from your minds. Present your needs to God in every form of prayer and petitions full of gratitude. Then God's own peace, which is beyond understanding, will stand guard over your hearts and minds in Christ Jesus.

Philippians 4:4-8

Rejoice because your names are registered as citizens of heaven.

Luke 10:20 (NLT)

I take joy in doing your will, my cry for your law is written on my heart.

Psalm 40:8 (NLT)

Always be joyful. Keep on praying. No matter what happens, always be thankful, for this is God's will for you who belong to Christ Jesus.

1Thessalonians 5:16-18 (NLT)

I have told you this so that you will be filled with my joy. Yes, your joy will overflow.

John 15:11 (NLT)

You love Him even though you have never seen Him. Do you do not see Him, You trust Him, and even now you are happy with glorious, inexpressible joy. Your reward for trusting Him will be the salvation of your soul.

1 Peter 1:8-9 (NLT)

The precepts of the Lord are right, giving joy to the heart. The commands of the Lord are radiant, giving life to the eyes.

Psalm 9:8

Give all your worries and cares to God, for He cares about what happens to you. Be careful! Watch out for the attacks from the Devil, your great enemy. He prowls around like a roaring lion, looking from some victim to devour. Take firm stand against him, and be strong in faith.

1 Peter 5:7-8 (NLT)

Don't worry about having enough food or drink or clothing. Why be like pagans who are so deeply concerned about these things? Your heavenly Father already knows all your needs, and He will give you all you need from day to day if you live for Him and make the kingdom of God your primary concern.

Matthew 6:31-34 (NLT)

Yet true religion with contentment is a great wealth. After all, we didn't bring anything with us when we came into the world, and we certainly cannot carry anything with us when we die. So if we have enough food and clothing, let us be content.

1Timothy 6:6-8 (NLT)

Choose good reputation over great riches, for being held in high esteem is better than having silver and gold.

Proverbs 22:1 (NLT)

"And this is the testimony: God has given us eternal life, and this life is in His Son. He who has the Son has life; he who does not the Son of God does not have life. I write these things to you who believe in the name of the Son of God so that you may know you have eternal life."

1 John 5:11-13

Since God choose you to be holy people whom He loves, you must clothe yourselves with tenderhearted mercy, kindness, humility, gentleness, and patience.

you make allowance for each other's faults and forgive the person who offends you. Remember the Lord forgave you, so you must forgive others.

Colossians 3:12-13 (NLT)

Those who obey my commandments are the one who love me. And because they love me, my Father will love them, and I will love them. And I will reveal myself to each one of them.

John 14:21 (NLT)

Thus says the Lord: Let not the wise man glory in his wisdom, nor the strong man glory in his strength, nor the rich man glory in his riches. But rather, let him who glories, glory in this, is his prudence he knows Me. Knows that I the Lord, bring about kindness justice and uprightness on earth, for with such am I pleased, says the Lord.

Jeremiah 9: 22-23

Let the words of Christ, in all their richness, live in your hearts and make you wise. Use His words to teach and counsel each other.

Colossians 3:16 (NLT)

Study this Book of the Law continually. Meditate on it day and night so you may be sure to obey all that is written in it. Only then will you succeed.

Joshua 1:8 (NLT)

Grow in the special favor and knowledge of our Lord and Savior Jesus Christ. To Him be glory and honor, both now and forevermore. Amen.

2 Peter 3:18 (NLT)

For the word of God is full of power. It is sharper than the sharpest knife, cutting deep into our innermost thoughts and desires. It exposes us for what we really are. Nothing in all creation can hide from Him. Everything is naked and exposed before His eyes. This is the God to whom we must explain all that we have done.

Hebrews4:12-13 (NLT)

Don't repay evil for evil. Don't retaliate when people say unkind things about you. Instead, pay them back with a blessing. That is what God wants you to do, and He will bless you for it.

1 Peter 3:9 (NLT)

So don't get tired of doing what is good. Don't get discouraged and give up, for we will reap a harvest of blessing at the appropriate time.

Galatians 6:9 (NLT)

Do not bring sorrow to God's Holy Spirit by the way you live. Remember, He is the one who has identified you as His own, guaranteeing that you will be saved on the day of redemption.

Ephesians 4:30 (NLT)

It is God who gives us, along with you, the ability to stand firm for Christ. He has commissioned us, and He has identified us as His own by placing the Holy Spirit in our hearts as the first installment of everything He will give us.

2 Corinthians 1:21-22 (NLT)

Don't you know that your body is the temple of the Holy Spirit, who live in you and was given to you by God? You do not belong to yourself.

Corinthians 6:19 (NLT)

Those who live only to satisfy their own sinful desires, will harvest the consequences of decay, and death. But who live to please the spirit will harvest everlasting life from the spirit.

Galatians 6:8 (NLT)

So get rid of all the filth and evil in your lives, and humbly accept the message of God has planted in your hearts, for it is strong enough to save your soul.

James 1:21 (NLT)

"Don't sin by letting anger gain control over you," don't let the sun go down while you are still angry. For anger gives a mighty foothold to the Devil.

Ephesians 4:26-27 (NLT)

But remember that the temptations that come into your life are no different from what others experience. And God is faithful. He will keep the temptation from becoming so strong that you can't stand up against it. When you are tempted, He will show you a way out so that you will not give in to it.

1 Corinthians 10:13 (NLT)

Put on salvation as your helmet, and take the sword of the spirit, which is the word of God.

Ephesians 6:17 (NLT)

Whatever you do, whether in speech or in action, do it in the name of the Lord Jesus. Give thanks to God the Father through Him.

Colossians 3:17

Those who listen to instruction will prosper those who trust in the Lord will be happy.

Proverbs 16:20 (NLT)

Above all, let your love for one another be constant, for love covers the multitude of sins.

1 Peter 4:8

Love each other with genuine affection, and take delight in honoring each other.

Romans 12:10 (NLT)

I pray that your love for each other will overflow more and more, and that you will keep on growing in your knowledge and understanding. For I want you to understand what really matters, so that you may live pure and blameless lives until Jesus returns.

Philippians 1:9-10 (NLT)

May our Lord Jesus Christ and God our Father, who loved us and in His special favor give us everlasting comfort and good hope, comfort your hearts give you strength in every good thing you do and say.

2 Thessalonians 2:16 (NLT)

Whenever we have the opportunity, we should do good to everyone, especially to our Christians brothers and sisters in Christ.

Galatians 6:10 (NLT)

Love does no wrong to anyone, so love satisfies all of God's requirements.

Romans 13:10 (NLT)

Christ said: I have loved you even as the Father has loved me. Remain in my love. When you obey me, you remain in my love, just as I obey my Father and remain in His love. I have told you this so that you will be filled with my joy. Yes, your joy will overflow!

John 15:9-11 (NLT)

Jesus said: "Don't let your heart be troubled. Trust in God. And trust in me. There are many rooms in my Father's house... I am going there to prepare a place for you, I will come back. Then I will take you to be with me so that you may be where I am.

John14:1-3 (NLT)

You can be sure that the more we suffer for Christ, the more God will shower us with His comfort through Christ.

2 Corinthians 1:5 (NLT)

You shall love the Lord your God with all your heart, with all your soul, with all your strength, and with your entire mind, and love your neighbor as yourself.

Luke 10:27

The purpose on my instruction is that all the Christians there would be filled with love that comes from a pure heart, a clear conscience, and sincere faith.

1Timothy 1:5 (NLT)

Blessed are those who trust in the Lord and have made the Lord their hope and confidence. They are like trees planted along the riverbank, with roots that reach deep into the water. Such trees are not bothered by the heat or worried by long months of drought. Their leaves stay green, and they go right in producing delicious fruit.

Jeremiah 17:7-8 (NLT)

Blessed be the name of God forever and ever, for He alone has wisdom and power.

Daniel 2:20

For every child of God defeats this evil world by trusting Christ to give the victory. And the ones who win this battle against the world are the ones who believe that Jesus is the Son of God.

John 5:4-5 (NLT)

God does not call us to immorality but to holiness.

1Thessalonians 4:7

Remember, Scriptures says, "Be holy for I am holy"

1 peter 1:15

The Lord saves the godly; He is their fortress in times of trouble. The Lord helps them, rescuing them from the wicked. He saves them and they find shelter in Him.

Psalm 38:39-40 (NLT)

We are pressed on every side of troubles, but we are not crushed and broken. We are perplexed, but we don't give up and quit. We are hunted down, but God never abandon us. We get knocked down, but we get up again and keep going. Through suffering, these bodies of ours constantly share in the death of Jesus so that the life of Jesus may also be seen in our bodies. All of these things are for your benefits. And as God's grace brings more and more people to Christ, there will be great thanksgiving, and God will receive more and more glory. That is why we never give up. Though our bodies are dying, our spirits are being renewed every day. For our present troubles are quite small and won't last very long. Yet produces for us an immeasurably great glory that will last forever! So don't look at the troubles we can see right now; we look forward to what we have not seen. For the trouble we seen will soon be over, but the joy to come will last forever.

2 Corinthians 4:8-10, 15-18 (NLT)

God blesses the people who patiently endure testing. Afterward they will receive the crown of life that God has promised to those who love Him.

James 1:12 (NLT)

Don't worry about anything; but pray about everything. Tell God what you need, and thank Him for all He has done. If you do this, you will experience God's peace, which is far more wonderful than the human mind can understand. His peace will guard your hearts and minds as you live in Christ Jesus.

Philippians 4:6-7 (NLT)

If you sinful people know how to give good gifts to your children, how much more will your heavenly Father give the Holy Spirit to those who ask Him?

Luke11:13 (NLT)

Call to me I will answer you, and I will tell you great and mighty things you do not know.

Jeremiah 33:3 (NLT)

Yes, the Lord pours down His blessing.

Psalm 85:12 (NLT)

Whatever good and perfect comes from God above.

James 1:17 (NLT)

If you need wisdom—if you want to know what God wants you to do—ask Him, and He will gladly tell you. He will not resent your asking. But when you ask Him, be sure that you really expect Him to answer, for a doubtful mind is unsettled as a wave of the sea that is driven and tossed by the wind. People like that should not expect to receive anything from the Lord. They can't make up their minds. They waver back and forth in everything they do.

James 1:5-8 (NLT)

You must each make up your own mind as to how much you give. Don't give reluctantly or in response to pressure. For God loves the person who gives cheerfully.

2 Corinthians 9:7-8 (NLT)

You need to recall the words of the Lord Jesus Himself said; there is more happiness in giving than receiving.

Acts 20:35

Give freely without begrudging it, and the Lord your God will bless you in everything you do.

Deuteronomy 15:10 (NLT)

Do you not realize that those who work in the temple are supported by the temple, and those who minister at the altar share the offerings of the altar? Likewise the Lord ordered that those who preach the gospel should live by the gospel.

1 Corinthians 9:13-14

I command you—be strong and courageous! Do not be afraid or discouraged. For the Lord your God is with you wherever you go.

Joshua 1:9 (NLT)

Be on guard. Stand true to what you believe. Be courageous. Be strong. And everything you do must be done in love.

1 Corinthians 16:13 (NLT)

Do what is right and good in the Lord's sight, so all will go well for you.

Deuteronomy 6:18 (NLT)

The Lord is close to the broken hearted; He rescues those who are crushed in spirit.

Psalm 34:18 (NLT)

Give your burdens to the Lord, and He will take care of you. He will not permit the godly to slip and fall.

Psalm 55:22 (NLT)

God is our refuge and strength, always ready to help in times of trouble.

Psalm 46:1 (NLT)

All praise to the Lord and God the Father of our Lord Jesus Christ. He is the source of every mercy and the God who comforts us. He comforts us in all our troubles so that we can comfort others. When others are troubled, we will be able to give them the same comfort God has given us. You can be sure that the more we suffer for Christ, the more God will shower us with His comfort through Christ. So when we are weighed down with troubles, it is for your benefit and salvation! For when God comforts us, it is so that we, in turn, can be encouragement to you. Then you can patiently endure the same things we suffer. You are confident that as you share in suffering, you will also share God's comfort.

2 Corinthians 1:3-7 (NLT)

Jesus said: "Come to Me, all of you who are weary and carry heavy burdens, and I will give you rest. Take my yoke upon you. Let me teach you, because I am humble and gentle, and you will find rest for your soul. For my yoke fits perfectly, and the burden I give you is light.

Matthew 11:28-30 (NLT)

The Lord is my rock, my fortress, and my savior, my God is my rock, in whom I find protection. He is my shield, the strength of my salvation, and my stronghold.

Psalms 18:2 (NLT)

Praise the name of the Lord forever and ever, for He alone has all wisdom and power.

Daniel 2:20 (NLT)

I have told you all this so that you may have peace in me. Here on earth you will have many trials and sorrows. But take heart, because I have overcome the world.

John 16:33 (NLT)

Whenever trouble comes your way, let it be an opportunity for joy. For when your faith is tested, your endurance has a chance to grow. So let it grow, for your endurance is fully developed, you will be strong in character and ready for anything.

James 1:2-4 (NLT)

But I know! I, the Lord, search all hearts and examine secret motives. I give all people their due rewards, according to what their actions deserve."

Jeremiah 17:10 (NLT)

Don't team up with those who are unbelievers. How can goodness be a partner with wickedness? How can light live with darkness?

2 Corinthians 6:14 (NLT)

All Scripture is inspired by God and is useful to teach us what is true and to make us realize what is wrong in our lives. It straightens us out and teaches us to do what is right. It is God's way of preparing us in every way, fully equipped for every good things God wants us to do.

2 Timothy 3:16-17 (NLT)

Don't just pretend that you love others. Really love them. Hate what is wrong. Stand on the side of the good. Love each other with genuine affection, and take delight in honoring each other. Never be lazy in your work, but serve the Lord enthusiastically.

Romans 12:9-11 (NLT)

God is love, and all who live in love live in God, and God lives in them. And as we live in God, our love grows more perfect. So we will not be afraid on the Day of Judgment, but we can face Him with confidence because we are like Christ here in this world.

1 John 4:16-17 (NLT)

Christ said: If you love me, obey my commandments. I will ask the Father and He will give you another counselor, who will never leave you. He is the Holy Spirit, who leads into all truth.

John 14:15-17 (NLT)

Remain in me, and I will remain in you. For a branch cannot produce fruit if it is severed from the vine and you cannot be fruitful apart from me. Yes I am the vine; and you are the branches. Those who remain in me, and I in them, will produce much fruit. For apart from me you can do nothing.

John 15:4-5 (NLT)

Those who love the law have great peace and do not stumble.

Psalm 119:165 (NLT)

Trust in God's unfailing love forever and ever.

Psalm 52:8 (NLT)

I take joy in doing your will, my God, for your law is written on my heart.

Psalm 40:8 (NLT)

What can we say about such wonderful things as these? If God is for us, who can be against us?

Romans 8:31 (NLT)

Trust in the Lord with all your heart; do not depend on your own understanding. Seek His will in all you do, and He will direct your paths.

Proverbs 3:5-6 (NLT)

My thoughts are completely different than yours," says the Lord. "And my ways are far beyond anything you could imagine. For just as heavens are higher from the earth, so are my ways higher than your ways and my thoughts higher than your thoughts.

Isaiah 55:8-9 (NLT)

Great is the Lord! He is most worthy to be praise! His greatness is beyond discovery.

Psalm 145:3 (NLT)

For with God nothing shall be impossible.

Luke1:37

For every child of God defeats this evil world by trusting Christ to give the victory. And the ones that who win this battle against the world are the ones who believe that Jesus is the Son of God.

1 John 5:4-5 (NLT)

For I can do everything with the help of Christ who gives me the strength I need.

Philippians 4:13 (NLT)

With Jesus help, let us continually offer our sacrifice of praise to God by proclaiming the glory of His name.

Hebrews 13:15 (NLT)

You have done many good things for me, Lord, just as you promised.

Psalm 119:65 (NLT)

Stay away from love of money; be satisfied with what you have. For God has said: "I will never fail you. I will never forsake you."

Hebrews 13:5 (NLT)

And how you benefit if you gain the whole world but lose your own soul in the process?

Mark 8:36 (NLT)

For wealth last not forever, nor even a crown from age to age.

Proverbs 27:24

Be intent on things above rather than on things on earth.

Colossians 3:2

...let us keep our eyes fixed on Jesus, who inspires and perfect our faith.

Hebrews 12:2

Don't be concerned about the outward beauty that depends on fancy hairstyles, expensive jewelry, or beautiful clothes. You will be known for the beauty that comes from within, the unfading beauty of a gentle quiet spirit.

1 Peter 3:3-4 (NLT)

Do not lay up for yourself treasures on earth... makes your practice instead to store up heavenly treasure. Remember, where your treasure is, there your heart is also.

Matthew 6:19-21

Teach your children to choose the right path, and when they are older, they will remain upon it.

Proverbs 22:6 (NLT)

If you refuse to discipline your children, it proves you don't love them; if you love your children, you will prompt to discipline them.

Proverbs 13:24 (NLT)

You children must always obey your parents, for this is what pleases the Lord.

Colossians 3:20 (NLT)

Children obey your parents because you belong to the Lord, for this is the right thing to do. "Honor your father and mother." This is the first of the Ten Commandments that ends with a promise: "you will live a long life, full of blessings."

Ephesians 6:1-3 (NLT)

For the whole law can be summed up in this one command: Love your neighbor as yourself.

Galatians 5:14 (NLT)

Love your enemy and do well, lend without expecting repayment...

Luke: 6:35

Do for others as you would have them do to you.

Luke 6:31

Stop judging others and you will not be judged. Stop criticizing others, or it will all come back to you. If you forgive others, you will be forgiven.

Luke 6:37 (NLT)

Be kind to each other, tenderhearted, forgiving one another, just as God through Christ has forgiven you.

Ephesians 4:32 (NLT)

In the same way, let your good deeds shine out for all to see, so that everyone will praise your heavenly Father.

Matthew 5:16 (NLT)

The harvest of justice is sown in peace for those who cultivate peace.

James 3:18

You must love the Lord your God with all your heart, all your soul, and all your strength. You must commit yourselves wholeheartedly to these commands.

Deuteronomy 6:5 (NLT)

Cheerfully share your home with those who need a meal or a place to stay.

1 Peter 4:9 (NLT)

Work hard and cheerfully in whatever you do, as though you are working for the Lord rather than for people.

Colossians 3:23 (NLT)

The Lord is the spirit, and wherever the spirit of the Lord is, He gives freedom.

2 Corinthians 3:17 (NLT)

Create in me a clean heart, O God. Renew a right spirit within me.

Psalm 51:10 (NLT)

Trust in the Lord and do good. Then you will live safely in the land and prosper. Take delight in the Lord, and He will give your hearts desires. Commit everything you do to the Lord. Trust Him, and He will help you.

Proverbs 37:3-5 (NLT)

For it is not those who hear the law who are just in the sight of God, it is those who will keep it who declare just.

Hebrews 2:13

In everything you do, stay away from complaining and arguing.

Philippians 2:14 (NLT)

But when the Holy Spirit controls our lives, He will produce this kind of fruit in us: love, joy, peace, patience, kindness, goodness, faithfulness, gentleness, and self control. Those who belong to Christ Jesus have nailed the passions and desires of their sinful nature to His cross and crucified them there. If we are living now by the Holy Spirit, let us follow the Holy Spirit's leading in every part of our lives.

Galatians 5:22-25 (NLT)

You will keep perfect peace all who trust in you, whose thoughts are fixed on you!

Isaiah 26:3 (NLT)

May the Lord bless you and protect you. May the Lord smile on you and be gracious to you. May the Lord shows you His favor and give you peace.

Numbers 6:24-26 (NLT)

Peace is my farewell to you. My peace is my gift to you. I do not give it to you as the world gives peace. Do not be distressed or fearful.

John 14:27

May God who gives patience and encouragement help you live in complete harmony with each other-each with the attitude of Christ toward the other. And then all of us can praise the Lord together with one voice, giving glory to God, the Father of our Lord Jesus Christ.

Romans 15:5-6 (NLT)

And I pray that Christ will be more and more at home in your hearts as you trust Him. May your roots, go down deep into the soil of God's marvelous love. And you may have the power to understand, as all God's people should, how wide, how long, how high, and how deep His love really is. May you experience the love of Christ though it so great you will never understand it. Then you will filled with the fullness of life and power that comes from God.

Ephesians 3:17-19 (NLT)

JESUS ACCEPTS YOU AS YOU ARE...

If God knocks on your heart

are you ready to listen?

Are you ready to accept what

God wants you to be?

Are you ready to serve Jesus

Christ our savior?

Have you put your trust in Him?

If your answer is "Yes" you are ready to receive Jesus. God wants His children to accept Him. It is your sincere desire, to invite Him to come into your heart as your personal Lord and Savior. Think about everything you have done wrong, confess your sins, and believe in your heart that Jesus died on the cross for your sins, and turn away from all your past sins. God wants to forgive your sins, give you life, peace, and a new beginning. Trust in what He says in His word. He wants to help you and He wants to guide you. Are you ready to accept the gift of eternal life?

Please say this prayer: Dear Jesus, I ask your forgiveness, and I receive you in my heart. I believe that you shed your precious blood and died for my sins. Today I accept your free gift of love, grace, mercy and peace. I am here now to repent and believe in You, the only Son of God. Help me to follow You, and share this wonderful news to everyone I meet. Thank you for forgiving me and giving me eternal life. Amen.

FAITH, HOPE, AND LOVE

In faith we grow.

In love we share.

In hope we endure.

Faith, hope, and love are our weapons today...

ABOUT THE AUTHOR

Mila Rayot is originally from the Philippines. She came from a family of twelve children. She is second to the youngest of the family. She was raised in a Christian home where biblical principles and the love of God reigned. She has been a Christian all her life. She chooses the way of Christ her savior and God direct her steps. If at anytime she can help, or if you need a piece of advice of anything, she is there to listen and to help. She discovers the joy of service without expecting in return, reward or praise. Mila is a mother of two daughters, named Tara and Cailin, and together with her husband Chris. She presently works for the State in Albany, New York.

SPECIAL THANKS

I want to thank God from the bottom of my heart, that I have parents who trust God's promises, and obey His guidance, believe the good news of eternal life through faith in Jesus Christ. I am incredibly blest to have them in my life.

I also want to extend my special thanks to my daughters, Tara and Cailin for helping me type my book. They have been supportive toward my work to get it done, so that I can spend more time with them. They are kind, giving, God-loving, and Bible-believing. I love you both very much!

I want to thank a person who deserves a special award of kindness and love, my husband Chris. He has spent a great deal of time editing my manuscript. He is been supportive, committed to the Lord, and committed to me for life. Chris and I share many common interests. Thanks for everything!

I want to send a special thanks to my friend Lalitha Iyer for always being there to help edit my manuscript. She took her time to help me, never asked anything in return. I want you to know how greatly appreciated you are.

I would also like to thanks Mike Foley and Kathy Romano, for sharing their artistic and creative talents. You both definitely put on the right touches, its beautiful illustrations. Once again, thank you for sharing your gift with so many. God bless you all!

To contact the author write:

Mila Rayot

P.O. Box 2069

Albany, New York 12220 0069

Internet Address: aurea@sonmedia.com

If you would like to share your Thoughts, Comments, Testimonies, Prayer Request, please feel free to write me at the above address.

LET ME REMEMBER...

Love means action and service.

LET ME REMEMBER...

LET ME REMEMBER...

LET ME REMEMBER...

LET ME REMEMBER...

LET ME REMEMBER...

LET ME REMEMBER...

LET ME REMEMBER...

LET ME REMEMBER...

PRAYER REQUEST

PRAYER REQUEST

PRAYER REQUEST

PRAYER REQUEST

PRAYER REQUEST

PRAYER REQUEST

PRAYER REQUEST

PRAYER REQUEST

PRAYER REQUEST

NOTES

NOTES

NOTES

NOTES

NOTES

NOTES

NOTES

NOTES

NOTES

Printed in the United States
35095LVS00005B/326